A Holiday Memoir

to Guernsey

Sherrie Lowe

Return to Guernsey
Published in 2025 by FeedARead.com Publishing
– Arts Council funded

First Edition

A CIP catalogue record for this title is available from the British Library.

Names of family and friends have been changed for privacy.

Cover Design and Formatting by The Book Khaleesi
www.thebookkhaleesi.com

Other Books by Sherrie Lowe

Memoirs

Shadow Across the Sun: A Memoir
Better or Dead: More Memoirs
My Furry Loves

Novels

Song of the Phoenix
The Author, The Gardener and The Woman What Does
Angel Breaths
Over A Spitfire
Over A Spitfire II: The Sequel
Whisper to Me

Willows Dip Series

A Lapse of Sanity - Book 1
After the Solstice - Book 2: The Sequel
Free Flight - Book 3
A Treasure Lost - Book 4
Not Reported Missing – Book 5
Don't Cough on Me – Book 6
Soul Saver – Book 7

Collections

Sonnets
Neighbourhood Watching – Willows Dip Shorts
The Journey
Just A Moment
A Treasury of Diverse Tales

Short Story

Love and Roses

Acknowledgements

My grateful thanks go to my wonderful family for both the Center Parcs and Guernsey holidays and all of their help with everything, I couldn't have done either without them.

To Tracey Sadler and her team at Albany Apartments, Guernsey for a fabulous and comfortable home from home.

To members of the Guernsey Facebook groups for their advice on getting around – invaluable. Also my lovely M.E friends in the Facebook group for their encouragement and support plus advice on travel, airport assistance etc.

To Sue and Sam at Milton Travel, Stoke-on-Trent for booking my flights and making sure my airport assistance ran smoothly and my two friends for recommending them and checking on release dates – they know who they are.

Aurigny Airlines, Guernsey for superb airport assistance and making my first flights so enjoyable and the airport staff at both Guernsey and Manchester airports.

To Steve's Travel, Stoke-on-Trent and his brother Brian for driving me to and from Manchester – perfect!

As always to The Book Khaleesi for their superb formatting and animated banner, and creating the fabulous cover from my photograph of St Peter Port, Guernsey, Channel Islands – I could never publish without them.

To feedaread.com for their usual excellent quality paperback and to Amazon KDP for the eBook format.

Many thanks to all.

To my family.
Treasure beyond measure.

Chapter 1

June 2023

"What's this about Mexico?" I texted my eldest son Matt on WhatsApp the day after the joint ninth birthday party for his daughter Rosie, my granddaughter, and his father, Barry, my ex husband's 70th at Matt and Helena's home.

"It's just an idea we had to save up and go again in about four years. We might even get married out there. Would you be up for it?"

I laughed as I sat in bed messaging on my phone. Mexico might be on Mars for the likelihood of me getting there.

Having suffered from M.E/C.F.S for nearly thirty years and the previous autumn, 2022, being almost bedbound with debilitating migraines I'd thought I was on a fast track to death never mind Mexico. However, I did nurture a dream, and I told him.

"No way could I ever manage Mexico but it's always been my dream to go back to Guernsey."

"Well what about for your 70th?"

I was sixty eight then and had no plans for my 70th. Barry had asked me at his birthday bash before he'd got hammered on Prosecco, "What are you doing for your 70th Sherrie?" and I'd replied, "I've absolutely no idea." To me it was just another birthday and after the last year I'd just be glad to be alive, but Guernsey? Was it possible? My dream island?

As for Matt and Helena getting married they'd been together since 2006, engaged since 2010, three beautiful children, a son and two daughters, Christian aged fifteen, Rosie now nine, Anna five, still as close as in their early days, but the wedding kept being put back. His brother Elliott had met Hayley in the primary school where they both taught in 2013 and beaten them to the altar in 2017; also parents to four year old Charlotte and Harry just coming up to his first birthday. Their wedding had been a wonderful family occasion and I offered up a silent prayer for Matt and Helena's wedding; 'Please not Mexico; somewhere I can get to.'

Replying to Matt I said, "I'd love to go back to Guernsey but I don't know if I could manage it."

"Well you're making good progress since Sara's diet plan. Leave it with me I'll have a word with Ace." (His brother's nickname.)

I put the phone down on the bed beside me and pondered. I *was* making good progress since Sara, my second cousin, a nutritional therapist, had put me on a diet plan.

As mentioned I'd suffered the most debilitating migraines the autumn of 2022 after being put on metformin for mild diabetes. I hadn't wanted to go on it; my sugar levels weren't that high but G.Ps had been banging on about pre diabetes for years – I'm sure they get funding for it – so I gave in. BIG MISTAKE!! I will *never* go on unnecessary medication again!

Likewise vaccines. The Moderna vaccine for Covid triggered three consecutive migraines as soon as I'd had it and I was ill for a fortnight, no problems with the first two which were AstraZeneca but we needed them to get the pandemic under control, but I digress.

From September 2022 to January 2023 I could barely see. Couldn't read, watch TV, listen to sounds, scroll on the phone. I did, minimally because living alone it was my link to the outside world, but every eye movement knocked me sick. I spent Christmas alone in bed, only sharing family photos. The boys and families visited separately for just long enough to exchange presents and the children had been warned to be quiet because I couldn't cope with noise – still can't to any extent and with M.E limitations I need to spend a lot of quiet time alone although it's not necessarily what I'd choose. I never left the house for six weeks and I thought this was it, galloping towards death. Then a strange thing happened.

The only times I get contacted through my website are for people wanting money; either to sell me something or to try and get me to part with cash for them to promote my books. I don't think so; I can do a better job myself. As I lay in bed, daring a few seconds glance at my phone a contact came up so I had a look. It read thus:

'Dream your dreams of Heaven. Ask Jesus the impossible.'

The impossible at that moment was to get out of bed, out of the house and visit the boys. I despaired of ever going to their houses again but I couldn't read anymore at that point so I put it aside and went back to it later. Basically she was trying to sell me her book about her near death experience. I wouldn't be buying as I couldn't read with the migraines, visual disturbances, couldn't do the side to side eye movement without feeling horribly nauseous and faint, but what leapt out to me was, 'Ask Jesus the impossible,' so I thought, 'OK, I'm asking.'

I'd fallen out with God many years before for giving me M.E after my divorce when I needed to work to provide for me and the boys who were then thirteen and eleven. How can you pray to someone and put your faith in them when they let you down? Maybe Jesus would be kinder. I did chat to the angels and perhaps Jesus was their boss? I could only ask.

The first positive step, I googled metformin and migraines and there was a link between them so I stopped taking it there and then. I noticed a slight improvement in my head. Next came New Year wishes to and from my cousin and she put me onto Sara, her daughter, who after I'd looked at her website, arranged genetic tests for me. The results showed various chemical imbalances in the brain and she devised a diet to balance them, tailored to my M.E capabilities; I can't prepare and cook meals, they have to be easy go-to meals that take little or no preparation for my energy levels or lack of them.

Alongside it she devised a diet to bring sugar levels down so I need never again resort to diabetic medication – which I was delighted to tell my doctor when it showed in my next blood test results! Over the next few weeks I managed tentative trips out to the local shop – very anxious not having driven for six weeks – and made it to the boys houses for two birthday parties, by taxi, my driving days to their homes were long gone anyway. From a fast track to death, Jesus had answered the impossible by guiding me off the metformin and to Sara.

Another strange thing came to mind later. In September 2021 I did an interview on BBC Radio Guernsey about my book Not Reported Missing, in which I had characters going there on holiday, and the D.J said to me, 'You need to get yourself back over here.' I thought never in a million years would I manage it but I said, 'Well the scientists are looking into Long Covid and likening it to M.E so if they come up with anything that would make it possible for me to travel, Guernsey would be top of my list.' Sara got me to the scientists.

Another comment was made by Christian as we sat chatting at Charlotte's birthday party. He said. "Would you be able to come to Center Parcs with us?"

I was very unsure. That was only my second visit out and I was still very anxious.

There is no cure for M.E. and when I set out on the diet plan with Sara my aim was to control the migraines and the diabetes and manage the M.E so that I was able to get out and perhaps have a holiday sometimes. My ask of Jesus was a life with my family.

Could I do Center Parcs? Could I do Guernsey?

It would be wonderful if I could, if we could all go together, that they could show me Center Parcs – their special place – and I could show them Guernsey – my special place.

Could I do it?

Chapter 2

When did Guernsey come back onto my radar? Fifteen? Twenty years ago? Perhaps it had never really been off.

A friend lent me the book, The Guernsey Literary and Potato Peel Pie Society. Healthspan sent their supplement catalogues and I noticed their address was St Peter Port, Guernsey, then later Helena sent thank you cards from the children from Moonpig and I saw the postmark and thought 'Oh Guernsey.'

Lots of little snippets like these I was drip fed and with each one the memory of the handsome, dark haired islander I'd gone on a date with when we were both nineteen and I was there on holiday came back. We wrote to each other for a while but our letters fizzled out. I regret not saving them and his photograph that he sent; I'd love to read them now, but I accepted when I got on the boat to come home that I'd never see him again. It wasn't what I wanted but what can you do?

C'est la vie.

I've never forgotten him and I never will. He's always had a special place in my heart and he always will.

That holiday happened by accident and is way up there as one of my best, although every holiday is special for the people you share it with, the places you see, the people you meet, the memories you make. It is covered in more detail in my first memoir, Shadow Across the Sun.

It was with the Methodist chapel youth club and my friend Louise said her younger brother had said there were some places left on the trip and did she and any of her friends want to go? At eighteen for her, nineteen for me, we were older than the others but yes please we'd like to go and I'm so so glad we did, so so grateful to her and her brother. It was one of the best experiences of my life and one of the most beautiful places. I fell in love with it as soon as I got off the boat – well once I'd got my jacket off that someone had been sick on as we'd hung over the rail of the open deck during the crossing enjoying the wind in our hair and the sea spray on our faces, but more about that in Shadow Across the Sun.

The first I'd heard of Guernsey were the tomatoes, boxes of them in Hanley market when I went with Mum as a child. White boxes with a smiling red tomato on saying Guernsey Toms. Little did I know of the fantastic holiday that awaited me there, years down the road.

The only other way I'd heard of the Channel Islands was through the 1970s TV series, Enemy at the Door, set in World War Two when the Germans occupied the islands but it never registered when I was there. I never associated that beautiful island with war, even though we visited the German Underground Military Hospital.

We weren't told anything about it on the visit, but then I wasn't near to our group leaders so maybe they had a bit of history, I just found it a very eerie place and was glad when we got out into the sunshine. I've learned a lot more in recent years from Google, YouTube, Facebook groups, TV programmes, books, and it must have been a terrible time for the islanders, those who stayed and those who were evacuated. I read a book recently by an islander whose family were evacuated to the UK and what a contrast their horrendous crossing of the channel as young children without their parents was to my joyful one as I went on holiday. People suffered dreadful experiences.

Mine though was wonderful and I always wanted to go back. As I wrote to my handsome date and thought of him in his beautiful island home, I knew it was impossible. Somewhere at the back of my mind though slumbered the timorous hope that sometime, someday, maybe I would go back. Not to him sadly, we both married others, but who knew it would take fifty one years?

Chapter 3

August 2023

Holiday time for both families; they were off to Center Parcs together. I was dog hotel for their dogs Rooney and Ralph. I'd never had them both together before but they were both getting on in years, I think eleven and eight or thereabouts, and only ever used to staying with me when their families were away so I couldn't have one and know that the other was in a kennel. We had a trial run, an overnight stay in the spring and it went well so I didn't forsee any problems.

They got on well, both good natured dogs, labradoodles, Rooney blond, Ralph black. I couldn't walk them because of my health limitations but whenever they stayed they were happy to sleep a lot! Elliott always said it was Ralph's spa retreat and he was very relaxed when he got home! We have a little sit outside in the garden if it's nice and they're OK, their needs are met. I'm exhausted by the end of the week and counting the hours but that's the physical bending and the change from my routine. They're nice to have for a few days and nice to give back. I love to see their delight when their families come for them. They're ecstatic.

Anyway their families dropped them off and said their goodbyes and we got down to the important business of treats and a wander in the garden to scent mark their spots and let all the visiting neighbourhood cats know that they were in charge of this patch for the week.

Fortunately Rooney and Ralph have different spots in the garden but there was a little bit of 'I'll have to go over yours,' more so from Rooney as he still had all his 'bits,' where Ralph had been separated from his as a puppy.

Matt had felt for him.

"Dunna cut his balls off," he'd said to Elliott.

"Well we think it'll be better for him in the long run," Elliott had replied, "testicular cancer and all that."

Some years later Matt and Helena had welcomed two beautiful Bengal kittens into their family, Apollo and Bruno who they did have separated from their tackle, but cats wander don't they – but I digress.

All settled into a pattern as it did when I had the dogs on their own. I let them on my bed for an hour night and morning while I'm having a cuppa but they have to get off when I sleep. Nobody shares my bed; I can't have fidgeting. Again their own beds are at opposite sides of my bed when they stay on their own, so no issues there.

"How's it going?" Matt texted the WhatsApp group later.

"All good," I replied, "Except for the fact that they're pooing machines!"

(Laughing emojis.)

"You're like Caesar Millan," Elliott said, he'd loved his programmes when he'd still lived at home with me or visited at later dates, "you've got a pack."

"Ha ha yes but it's nothing I haven't done before but I was a lot younger and fitter when we had Sheba and Jodi." They'd been my beautiful sable and white rough collies, mother and daughter, long gone over rainbow bridge but they all leave pawprints on our hearts don't they. "Brings back memories. We'll see how it goes over the week."

It went well, albeit said pooing machines seemed to think every time I let them out for a quick wee, 'Oh we might as well find a bit while we're here,' I must have kept Sainsbury's in poo bags!

The weather was quite pleasant so we sat out for a while most days and I thought about Guernsey. On nice sunny days I wanted to go, a little walk on the beach, feel the sand between my toes, paddle in the sea. In the cold of winter though I wouldn't want to go. I don't do winter. I just want to burrow down in my little den and wait for it to pass; the cold and the dark. I had had a look at a few places to stay in Guernsey and the one I was most drawn to were self catering apartments, which had previously been a hotel with a disco where I'd met my date.

I was drawn to them for that reason first and foremost, the memories, but also because they were quite central to St Peter Port, easily accessible from what I could remember, and I thought self catering would be better for all of us. That was what they were doing this week at Center Parcs, and for me it would be better for Sara's diet, plus I had stomach issues.

It all seemed so daunting though. It had been years since I'd booked any holiday, in the UK even and I'd never flown. I didn't have the first idea of how to book flights, let alone for ten of us. Perhaps it was all too much. Perhaps I wouldn't bother. I wouldn't want to go when I thought about it when it was cold in winter anyway. I'd said to Matt once a couple of years earlier after I'd done the radio interview and we'd sat in his garden, I go on and off the idea of Guernsey. Besides, I couldn't gauge the family's feelings, who wanted to go and who didn't. I knew Matt was up for it, it had been his idea, but I didn't know about anyone else. I couldn't think about it anymore.

Midweek came and disaster struck. I let the dogs out for last wee at 8.30 p.m, I go to bed at nine, email, Facebook etc on my phone, cuppa and ginger biscuit, wind down. They know this routine. It was summer so it was still light – thankfully! They went on a massive poofest!!

One each, I thought great, that's done, my gardener was due the next morning to mow the lawns so I needed to pick it up. Out I trotted armed with poo bags, did the necessary, turned round and there they were, in position doing another! Then another!!

"Nooo! Please no more!!" I wailed. There might have been a few sentence enhancers thrown in there as I surveyed the malodorous design decorating the lawn from top to bottom; my back splitting in two from all the bending. I went about my task muttering and cursing, all the while semi conscious of two pairs of soulful brown eyes observing my every move as if to say, 'Why are you angry? When we've got to go we've got to go and it's where we should go, not all over the lounge carpet.'

I wasn't moved by their mournful expressions even though they looked a mite apologetic for reasons they didn't understand. I just grunted, "Come on in then if you've finished and you can have your biscuits."

My gardener arrived the next day to a clean lawn, unaware of the drama of the previous evening to restore it to that condition, and provided the entertainment for the dogs as they watched through the window this strange wheeled beast gobbling up the grass. Even more interesting as he had to come through the house down the hall to the back garden and gave them a friendly knock and hello on the glass door, which they replied with a not so friendly frenzied barking session.

Later they had a surprise when my sister arrived with treat sticks for them when she'd been shopping. They were those soft types with something tasty down the middle. They greeted her like The Messiah, or a long lost friend. Rooney always pleaded with any visitors, 'Take me home, take me home!' I don't think he realized if they took him anywhere it would be to their home which would be far more strange to him than mine so he was best staying put! Anyway the treat sticks were more than adequate compensation for not being rescued.

During the afternoon Ralph kept making forays into the other room and when I checked up on him there he was in the kitchen waiting by the treats, worrying them to death.

"No you're not having another stick today," I told him. "I don't want another poofest. You can have one tomorrow then there's one each for you to take home."

He put his head on one side and listened. Of course he understood every word I said!

Friday arrived as I was evermore exhausted and Elliott was coming for Ralph so that was one dog less. Matt was coming for Rooney on the Saturday and the plan was to take me back with him for Christian's 15th birthday party at their house. It wasn't looking good. My back was weak from all the bending, stemming from Wednesday's poofest and I was running on empty. I could barely stay out of the recliner chair and wouldn't be able to sit on a different chair; definitely not anything upright such as a dining chair. I'd be devastated if I couldn't go. To miss going for a general visit upset me; to miss a birthday party would plunge me into black manic depression. This M.E let me down at every turn and the post exertional malaise that followed even the slightest overdoing anything be it mental or physical sometimes took a couple of days to hit and could last for several days, weeks, months even.

Elliott came for Ralph and that eased the workload but I wasn't feeling any better when I got up on Saturday to let Rooney out and I knew I wouldn't be able to make it to the party. Christian came with Matt to pick him up so I could give him his presents but we were all disappointed. When they left, even though the black cloak of depression descended it wasn't quite as suffocating as it might have been because I just relaxed in my own space and much as I was so disappointed not to be able to go I had at least seen them and I looked forward to a long soak in the bath, something I don't do when I've got the dogs, only have a quick dip because I don't like them out of my sight.

A few days later when I'd recovered, Matt called with the children, and a proposition.

"Do you want to come to Center Parcs with us in December? It's really good and Christmassy with all the lights and the kids go and see Santa."

I had been thinking of what I'd say if they asked me. "Who's going?"

"Helena's parents, and Dad." Elliott and Hayley wouldn't go because it was term time and they were both teachers.

Who goes on holiday with their ex? I said as much to Matt.

"Well it's a family holiday and he's their granddad."

"But he's my ex."

"You get on OK."

"Only as far as family occasions."

"Well we'd like you both to come."

I thought about it. "I'd have to have my own lodge anyway. I can't be with people for long, I need lots of alone, quiet time, I can't cope with noise."

"That won't be a problem. We'll all have a lodge together and get you one close by."

"What about walking? I can't do it. You said they had mobility scooters."

"They do. We'll hire one for the week. So will you come?"

I thought. "Yes I think so. I would love to but get the details and give me a few days and get back to me."

The children had listened with great interest, especially Christian as it had been his suggestion earlier in the year and he said, "It'll be a trial run for Guernsey for you without the flight."

A few days later Matt texted back with details and he and Helena booked it. He then replied with a gif of Borat saying, 'I am very excite!' and underneath, "Bloody hell we're going on holiday!"

It would be my first in twenty five years!

Chapter 4

December 2023
Center Parcs

Sara was delighted I was feeling well enough to go to Center Parcs thanks to her diet. She herself had suffered from M.E. for five years following a viral infection which had prompted her to publicize her story on her website to help others and how I'd got back in touch with her. As I've said there is no cure for M.E and lots of research is going on to try and find one but through her knowledge of diet, foods, contact with genetic tests, Sara has recovered, although she has to take care of her health, lots of aspects involved, watching stress levels etc. I am twenty years older than her and been ill for thirty years and I haven't had the recovery that she has but my aim when I set out on her diet was to control the diabetes and migraines and to try and manage the M.E more effectively to enable me to have some kind of a life with my family. Center Parcs would be a huge achievement. I'd also told her of my tentative ideas for Guernsey, where she'd been herself.

"Send me a photo of you in the pool," she'd said excitedly. She'd also added. "We'll get you to Guernsey Sherrie."

"Look who's proper excited!"

Matt sent me a photo of Rooney sitting expectantly in his bed in the back of their seven seater Audi as Matt was loading the car on the Monday morning we were due to go. Helena's parents were taking some of their luggage with them in their car to make room for me and mine, Rooney and his bed and food, so they were all getting started early whilst I paced myself to conserve my energy for the day. Mornings were always my weakest time and I needed to budget my energy carefully to be able to do the activities I wanted to do with them through the week; use too much too soon and it would kill all my plans.

I wanted to go to the pool which would be the following day, Tuesday. I'd had a new swimsuit – the first in many years, monochrome with black shorts – and I hoped it would look OK for the photo for Sara. If not for her I wouldn't be going, impossible. I'd been bedbound only a year ago with migraines but now I was going to be leaving the house for a whole five days!! Something I'd never have dreamed of. Ask Jesus the impossible the email had said.

The other activity I wanted to join them in was the pottery painting, which was booked for Wednesday.

They always painted a piece as a memory of each holiday and had sometimes done one for me, which I thought was so thoughtful during their holiday. They were a Nemo fish that Christian had painted when he was three years old, a gingerbread man plate that he'd painted some years later which I use for my cups for upstairs drinks, and Helena painted an owl mug which I daren't use for fear of breaking it! All beautiful. All treasured. I also have a turtle that Helena painted for me when she and Matt were first together and they'd gone with her family to Mexico, equally treasured. I wanted my own little piece to add to my collection.

Although growing up in The Potteries area of Stoke-on-Trent I'd done very little in the way of pottery painting other than small items that my beloved Auntie Eth, (Sara's grandma) had brought for me and my sister from her work as a paintress in a pottery factory, or potbank as they were known locally. One item we painted over and over was a little house with a lawn and path with an open doorway and chimney. It was an ashtray and as you put a cigarette in – my dad smoked as did lots of people then – the smoke came out of the chimney. We loved it! She had given us one each, along with lots of other gifts, owl money boxes, Carrot Cottage, a little house lamp with rabbits in, a mushroom house with bears in, both of which we still have to this day, treasured gifts from childhood. I couldn't wait to have a go at painting myself.

I laughed at Rooney looking so excited. It would be good that he was coming on holiday with us. He was going to come to my lodge on the Tuesday evening when they all went to the sports hall to watch the football. I wouldn't go; I'd be resting and pacing for the next day.

They arrived to pick me up at 11 a.m. and we were all as excited as Rooney! Matt took a picture of us in the car and off we set. It seemed strange to be waving good-bye to my little house for five days. I was a bit anxious about leaving it as it had been so long since I had – pre WIFI days so I'd turned that off! Well the hub gets hot doesn't it. My neighbours were keeping an eye on it for me, we look out for each other, and my sister and brother in law were going to drive past when they were out. I'd done it so many times in the past, it had just been so long ago.

We had a brief stop at McDonald's for lunch then continued on. It was quite familiar to them but all new to me. Not a long journey, about an hour and forty five minutes and we joined the queue to get into the parc. We pulled up to check in and were given our armbands.

"Can we get a second one for (whatever my number lodge was)" Matt asked the attendant, and turning to me he added, "in case you die," and we all laughed.

It all happened quite quickly then. Everywhere was very busy; I was worried how far I'd have to walk from the car park to get the mobility scooter but Matt found a space fairly close to, then we went to pick up the scooter.

I'd never used one before but it was quite easy and quite fun and would be my legs for the week. Matt took in all the details of how to charge it so I left it to him, he could explain it to me later. After that we made our way over to Starbucks where we joined Helena's parents.

We were very lucky with the weather for December,

azure blue skies and fluffy cotton wool ball white clouds, a bit of a nip in the air but not too bad and we were able to sit outside which was good because of Rooney. The seat on the scooter was much more comfortable, warmer and padded than those at the tables – well for a while! Matt was dying to get his hands on it!

"Can I have a go?" he asked.

Of course I said yes and we all laughed as he shot off up the bank and round the corner out of sight. Being unfamiliar with the place I'd no idea where he'd gone or for how long but he was soon back having enjoyed a little spin on my chariot.

Helena's brother and his girlfriend had also booked for the week so they joined us too and we sat there until it was time to go and find our lodges. Luckily they'd been able to get one for me next door but one to theirs, so I was nice and close; I could see it from my front door.

With the short December days and the cloud having gathered, dusk had flung its cloak over the pine forest as we made our way along the paths but we were able to get some photos of the children by the illuminated tree and I'd taken some of the huge sleigh and reindeer by Starbucks so the holiday had begun!

The scooter was fab! I loved it! It would be no good for home, my little Ford Fiesta, Bev was my chariot there and she had to go on as long as I would, but for here it was superb and made this holiday possible for me. Sherwood Forest swallowed us up as we looked for the numbers of our lodges. Presently we found them and although a little early and they were being checked over, we were allowed in. The supervisor if that's who she was assured me that the scooter would be absolutely fine left outside with its rain cover on and Matt put it on charge and went to join his family, leaving me to get acclimatized in my home for the week.

It was lovely! Just nice for one person or a couple: small round dining table and chairs, two seater settee, patio doors looking over the fields through the pine trees with a carpet of russet autumn leaves, there was a patio table and chairs and a covered barbeque but I wouldn't be needing those at this time of year; a wonderful view though to look over when I was sitting resting. There was a TV but I wouldn't be putting that on. I couldn't watch much with my weird head anyway and nothing I couldn't catch up on at home. Through the doorway was a very comfortable looking double bed. On the walls in both rooms were beautiful canvasses of the forest in various seasons and on the blackboard an exquisite chalk drawing of a red squirrel on a branch saying, 'Welcome to Winter Wonderland' which I took a picture of immediately. Then I just had a first cup of tea and something to eat and relaxed. I would be very comfortable here for the week.

After my cuppa and a rest I familiarized myself with the kitchen appliances. I cast a wary eye over the small dishwasher. I'm not acquainted with such an object. I opened the door and closed it again. That was all I'd be having to do with that. It was like an alien being. I'd never had any desire to have one and never will. Many years ago my then sister in law had wanted to off load her old one onto us and have us cut up our newly installed fitted kitchen to accommodate it! No thank you very much! I didn't want one under any circumstances and most certainly not for someone else's convenience, that's the purpose of the scrap metal men.

Microwave came next. Although I couldn't live without this piece of equipment at home I doubted I'd be becoming big buddies with this one here. Too high up for a start. I'd probably tip the soup all over my head if I tried to heat it up and get it out of that. I was at the back of the queue when they gave out height and my former five foot one inch has probably shrunk a bit with age so the microwave at that towering level was a no. The cooker I didn't look at. My own at home if I were to use the main oven I'd have to get the manual out to find out how to. Sara's diet was tailored to easy to prepare meals and for this week I'd do just that. The kitchen appliances here could have a holiday of their own.

Tuesday

I'd like to say I woke after a good night's sleep but hey ho not so. I'd gone to sleep on a high after having such a good day the day before and despite having a zopiclone sleeping pill that my doctor had prescribed with much reluctance, I'd woken at 2 a.m. for the loo and lay looking at the inside of my eyelids from then. I looked on WhatsApp around 6 a.m to see if Matt had been on but he hadn't so I didn't send a good morning message in case I woke any of them if his phone wasn't on silent so I went and made a cuppa and had a ginger biscuit, my kick start to the day, took them back to bed and texted Emily my sister. It's usually email for our morning and evening missives but it was eating up my data so text was better. Her sleeping pattern is even worse than mine so there's often a good chance she's awake somewhere along the line. She was so we had a little chat then a bit later Matt came on with, 'Morning Shuffs, (nickname from when I was forty because they said I shuffled in my slippers!!?) how did you sleep?'

'Crap, how about you?'

He'd done better but I think everyone takes time to settle in a different bed and he said he'd bob in when they went out for their first thing coffee, he, Christian and Barry. Today was swimming day and I was looking forward to christening my new swimsuit. I hadn't worn such an outfit in a long time and how I'd feel about exposing so much flesh I didn't know but it was quite a good disguise of all manner of sins and I liked it, an attractive black and white design with separate shorts so I was looking forward to taking it for a dip, not forgetting the photo for Sara.

The men bobbed in as promised to see if I wanted anything to eat or drink, which I didn't dare to with my unpredictable insides, best stick to what I'd brought with me, so off they went and said when we'd head off to the pool. It was good to know that Matt could just knock on the door and come in with his wrist band that he'd obtained in case I died!! Quite a comfort.

At the arranged time we set off, me on the scooter, it really was an ace machine! The weather was a bit murky but it didn't matter we'd be inside. I'm always a bit worried about how much walking and how much of my limited energy it will use and it seemed quite a way from parking the scooter outside to getting to the changing rooms inside, then finding an empty locker after we'd changed. The one facing me was 22, my number, that number follows me everywhere, I must see it a dozen times a day, or 222, angel numbers I'm told, so I aimed for that.

"No that's taken," said Helena.

"Have this one, 18 and share with Dad," said Matt.

I didn't want to share with Barry. If he was dithering about after, not wanting to leave when I did, or taking ages to make up his mind my energy would be dwindling, I needed one on my own.

"There isn't one," insisted Matt. "Share with Dad."

What was his game? He'd already got us coming on the family holiday together, now he'd got us sharing a locker. I told my online bestie in our communications later and we laughed. She said, 'It's like a Brian Rix farce, the adult children trying to throw their divorced parents together.' No hope of that. Barry and I got on well enough for family events but that was as far as it went – for the sake of family.

We reached poolside and they bagged their regular spot as I'd seen from their photos of previous holidays and it was lovely to be there with them even if I was on autopilot from my four hours sleep. I couldn't wait to get in the water for a swim. The girls were off straight away and we adults got acclimatised and chatted and everyone did their own thing.

"Do you want to do this photo for Sara?" Matt asked me.

"Yes OK then we won't forget."

Off we went, I posed in the water up to my knees, he took a couple of snaps then went back to our seats with my phone leaving me to splash around a bit.

It had been many years since I'd swam but it was like riding a bike, you didn't forget, so, full of confidence, I struck out with great aplomb in a magnificent breast stroke and promptly went right under!! I gasped and spluttered in horror and turned frantically over onto my back to float which I did succeed in doing, much to my relief! How could I not swim? I did manage a few little arm wiggles after that but didn't dare risk taking my feet off the bottom and thought well best get out now, the new cozzie had had a taster of the water, that would do until Guernsey, where I would be staying in the shallow end of the pool and by the bar!!

I cast a furtive glance round me to see if anyone had witnessed my near drowning but everyone seemed to be displaying their own water skills with their families much better than I, so I slunk out and back to my seat and wrapped my new beach towel around me, another acquisiton I hadn't needed in twenty five years.

Thankfully Barry was ready to leave when I was so no problems with the locker, although I think it was a bit early for everyone else but I can't last too long, I just hoped I didn't cramp their style too much.

In the evening, Matt, and family brought Rooney to my lodge while they went to the sports hall to watch the football on the big screen.

Anna exclaimed, "Nana Shuffs, your house is tiny!"

She was right; I suppose it was compared to theirs, which I hoped to go and see later in the week but for that night I just hoped to sleep once they'd come back for Roon.

Wednesday

Sadly the sleep wasn't much better. I made it to 4 a.m and that was it. Today was pottery painting day, which I really wanted to do but I knew I was pushing myself. I should have had a rest day but it would have to wait until tomorrow.

Matt and Helena had taken the girls to see Santa in the morning and I made my way on my trusty chariot to meet him at a designated point somewhere near the village square; I was getting to know my way around a little bit, I knew we turned somewhere near a phone box! He was there waiting for me which I was relieved about. I was surprised at how dependent I'd become on him. Living alone at home I was very independent. Having been divorced for almost thirty years I'd got quite used to doing most things for myself, either that or sourcing someone to pay to do them for me if I was unable, so to find myself so suddenly thinking, 'Matt will do it,' as with charging my scooter, came as a bit of a shock to me. I didn't know if I liked it or not.

"All right Shuffs?" he greeted me and I replied that I was and had the girls enjoyed their visit to The Great Man?

They had and we made our way to join them, Helena and Christian in the pottery place.

They knew the routine off by heart having done it so many times on previous holidays; they always painted a piece as a memento of every stay, so I just followed on as we chose which piece we wanted to paint from among the plain white pottery figures arranged on the shelves. I knew what I wanted immediately, a robin sitting on a branch with space for a tea light candle in it. I'd had robins successfully nest in my greenhouse in spring and seen two babies fledge, a wonderful experience, so my choice was easy. Anna chose a unicorn, Rosie two gnomes that she said were her mum and dad, Christian chose a Rudolph style reindeer, Helena a disk Christmas tree ornament and Matt a cereal bowl. We all went to our allotted table and they showed me which paints to use and said they would all come out darker when they were glazed and fired.

Growing up in The Potteries area of Stoke-on-Trent, Staffordshire, I felt I should have had some idea of pots but I'm ashamed to say I had none, never having worked in the industry so it was all new to me apart from the figures I'd painted as a child that Auntie Eth had brought home for Emily and I. We soon all became engrossed in our painting, just casting a glance at each other's work. Helena sat opposite me and she'd got each of the children, her and Matt to put a fingerprint on her ornament and made reindeer faces out of them, very creative! She also painted, 'Center Parcs 2023' on it. A lovely keepsake. Christian sat next to me and his reindeer was very intricate but not close to being finished by the time our hour was up! We had to then take them to the counter but once again I left it to Matt because my energy was dwindling fast on so little sleep and not budgeting it properly with rest days, I also wanted to have a look in the souvenir shop next door for something for my own little Christmas tree then I needed to get back to my lodge. Helena and the girls left, 'See you in twenty years when you've finished,' Rosie said to Christian as they went to the shop. I went to look for my ornament for my tree from next door, found a pretty glitter edged swan, then Matt came and saw me to the point where he'd met me then returned to Christian who would have added his finishing touches by then hopefully!

Dusk was gathering by this time and there was a light mist cloaking the pine forest. It was atmospheric and the author in me could feel a setting for a story as I traversed the road, but I was just conscious of my failing energy and couldn't push the scooter to go fast enough to get back. I was so relieved to see the number of my lodge, park and cover the scooter and go in and make a cup of tea and have something to eat and rest. Anxiety was setting in as well because I didn't feel well anymore. I'd so wanted to feel my best for the whole week and if I'd slept properly and paced I would have but with only a few hours sleep and pushing myself to do the activities I wanted to do with my family, it was taking its toll. Tomorrow would definitely have to be a rest day. I'd stay in the lodge and write to my friend Carmel, we wrote weekly and I could post it to her when I got home.

Thursday

As I'd promised myself I had a rest day and stayed in the lodge. Matt popped in as he'd done each morning and it was lovely to have him do that; see him every day, I'd miss that when I got home. They were going swimming again that day and in the evening they were going to look at the lights in the centre of the parc but I couldn't manage it, I was too weak, I wouldn't even be able to manage to walk the short distance across to have a look at their lodge that I'd hoped to do, Christian was going to send me a video of it. I was trying not to panic, to keep the anxiety under control, but I just wanted to go home and I was worrying how I was going to cope with the Friday which would be an early start for me – out at 10 a.m. – and a long day, pancakes weren't booked until 2 p.m. I was annoyed with my own body for letting me down. It was the first holiday I'd had in twenty five years, saved and spent money on and now I was wanting to go home. I didn't want to spend any part of my holiday wanting to go home!

As it turned out it was the best day weather wise, after Monday, the only day with some sunshine so I sat watching a tractor working backwards and forwards across the field outside the boundary.

The autumn leaves shone russet and gold in the sunlight and the blue sky with its puffball white clouds peeked through the towering pines beyond my window.

A couple of squirrels ran up and down the trees with expert precision and how I wished I had their agility and energy. A tiny chaffinch foraged in the earth beneath the leaves looking for food and it was pleasant to just sit and observe nature going about its everyday life with me as the visitor.

I took more photos to remember the view from my room for the special album of this trip when I got back home. I like proper prints in proper albums. I don't trust technology not to eat them!

Friday

Early start to be out of the lodges by 10 a.m. The men had gone to get the cars from the car park and the loading up began. Matt had the bright idea of using the scooter to take my bags to the car – he loved having a go of it; I hope he never comes to need one himself but you never know as we all age, he's got a football injury to his knee – and it did save time and leg work. I was very apprehensive and trying to keep the anxiety under control because if that escaped its cage and ran amok I'd be in a far worse situation and it would rob what little energy I had. The plan was to get to the sports hall then Matt would return the scooter which had to be back to be charged up ready for the next visitors, then we'd all stay in there until it was time to leave for pancakes at two.

We congregated on the path to begin the walk – ride for me – to the sports hall, Helena and her family along with Rooney on his lead, minus her dad who along with Matt had gone to return the cars to the car park. Barry stood there with his badminton racquet cocooned in its case, cradled lovingly in his arms. He was all but caressing it like a lover.

"I'll be needing this later," he informed me as I sat like Madge from the Benidorm series on the scooter but minus her gusto and venom, I was more like a wilted dandelion and in no mood for polite conversation, my efforts were all focused on staying upright and propelling my trusty chariot forwards. I cast him a glance that Catherine Tate's Lauren character would have been proud of, a withering stare of total indifference before turning my attention back to the road. How I made it to the sports hall is nothing short of a miracle and it seemed to pass in a blur as I followed everyone else on autopilot.

When we arrived Matt took the scooter back, Helena enquired where we could sit with the dog and was told anywhere uncarpeted. Rooney was very well trained anyway and never did anything indoors. We found seats and I wilted once more. I didn't dare have a drink because I'd need the toilet and I didn't have the energy to walk to them. Rooney got lots of attention from passers by which he enjoyed but his eyes never left Helena, whom he adored, he especially didn't want her to leave him in this strange place. One young girl fussed him as she passed and commented, 'I love your dog.'

Eventually I had to make the marathon trek to the loo. I'd brought my own drink of milk with me to keep sipping, along with a supply of cheese spread sandwiches and mint Viscount biscuits to keep the sugar levels balanced. I asked Matt where they were.

"Just over there," he indicated, directly opposite the hall to where we were sitting, opposite the badminton courts etc which they'd got booked for a game later. "It's not far. Go out of here, turn left, left again and it's just over there."

Not far for him, it was like the length of seventeen football pitches for me but I set off on my intrepid adventure and was thankful that there wasn't a queue. By the time I got back my energy was coming up a bit and I had a snack to help it on. Matt, Barry, Christian and the girls went for their game of badminton and Helena, her parents and I sat and watched and chatted.

"Where is it you want to go for your 70th?" she asked me.

"Guernsey. Are you up for it?"

"Yeah, we don't mind, we'll go anywhere. When were you thinking?"

"Well it would have to be school holiday time with Elliott and Hayley teaching so perhaps May half term? Only thing with that though is the apartments I'd looked at it said the pool wasn't open until June as it's outdoors, unless the weather's good."

"How about summer holidays then? The pool would definitely be open then."

"Could do. I don't mind. Whatever anyone agrees to."

"See what they think then."

We left it at that but I was pleased that she was interested because at that point the only one I'd got a positive response from had been Matt so I wasn't sure whether or not it would be happening. Elliott and Hayley liked to go on holiday on their own, which was understandable and I wouldn't normally commandeer anyone's holiday but with Matt suggesting it and it always having been my dream to go back, plus I'd always wanted to take Matt and Elliott but had then got ill so it hadn't happened, perhaps now was the only chance I'd have. Christian had seemed keen when we'd mentioned it but I wasn't sure about anyone else. I wouldn't push it, just see how it went; there was time yet.

They finished their game and it was soon time to move to the pancake house. Too far for me to walk so Matt called for one of the onsite mini buses and we parents went in that whilst the younger ones walked with Rooney. When we got there Christian took control, very confidently and said we had a table booked and asked if we were allowed to bring the dog in but we were told no, he'd have to stay outside. Thankfully it was a dry day and not too cold so we took turns sitting outside with him. He'd been such a good boy and seemed to have enjoyed being with his family. Helena's mum said he'd enjoyed the food! She loved cooking and made superb meals which I was always so disappointed I couldn't eat the more spicy dishes with my temperamental innards but I used to love her bacon rolls that she used to take to watch Christian play football on Sunday morning! I could well understand that Rooney had loved the food! Sadly I didn't dare risk having pancakes either because my stomach often took umbridge to eggs and we had an almost two hour drive home after we'd left there so I couldn't chance any shenanigans so I just had chocolate ice cream, a bit cold as it was winter but I'd still got my supply of sandwiches for the day. Everyone else's pancakes looked delicious and my mind could have devoured them but my digestive system said don't even think about it, you just stick to the tried and trusted sandwiches!

As everyone finished, time came to leave and we set off for home. The sun was setting, casting the sky with a glorious crimson glow through the pine forest as we drove out of the parc and onto the road.

"Bye Center Parcs," Rosie said wistfully and we all settled comfortably in our seats as Matt drove on.

The children soon fell asleep, Anna resting against my arm, and as I looked at them I envied them and how I remembered doing that as a child. If I did it now I'd wake up feeling like hell, my head feeling as though it had done a few turns in a tumble dryer. It was a pleasant drive back, seeing all the Christmas lights in homes and shops that we passed on the way. Matt dropped Helena and the children and Rooney off at home first and unloaded their bags as their house was closest, then he took me home.

It had been a lovely week; lovely to be with them and see their special place. I was only disappointed that I'd felt ill for the second part. It's true what they say; it's lovely to go traveling but always good to get home. It was the first time I'd been away in twenty five years, except for an overnight stay for Elliott and Hayley's wedding, and I had so missed my little home but perhaps if I got used to a holiday here and there I wouldn't miss it quite as much with each time. I'd seen their special place now, and I was looking forward to showing them mine in 2025.

The year ended on a good note with a wonderful Christmas, our usual Boxing Day celebrations at Elliott and Hayley's home, that I'd missed the previous year when I'd been in bed with migraines, so I was more than happy to be with my family for this one and offered up several thank yous to Jesus for yet more impossibles made possible.

Chapter 5

If I had to sum up 2024 in one word it would be challenging! After much ado I booked Albany Apartments in Guernsey, which had been Birnam Court Hotel back in 1974 which had had the disco where I'd met my date and it would be lovely to relive the memories being almost on the spot. It would be surreal to think that the last time I'd been there had been with him fifty one years ago and been so happy. The lady taking the reservations had been very understanding and helpful of my dithering around with dates and I wondered if she was used to people being a nuisance!

I'd suggested Albany Apartments to the family for several reasons. For me personally it was the memories. More practical reasons were, it was central to St Peter Port, I remembered it vaguely, to my thoughts it was quite flat for my walking difficulties, and self catering would suit us all. Besides that they were lovely apartments with an outdoor pool and gardens.

Getting a date to suit us all was proving more difficult. The lovely lady who answered my emails said if it was anything like trying to get her family together it was like herding cats. Eventually we all agreed on dates.

Next came flights. I'd never flown let alone booked one – nevermind for ten of us!! Two of my much travelled friends were very helpful in checking when they were released and advising of a local travel agent, who I booked through in the end. It was just unfortunate they were released after I'd had the week from hell with Cadent, gas supplier, forcing – bullying – me to have my gas meter moved, which I didn't want, then refusing to connect the pipework. After several unpleasant phone calls and threats of Trading Standards they agreed to do it as a goodwill gesture! And so they should! I never wanted the damn thing moving in the first place and to leave a vulnerable disabled old woman with no heating or hot water for four days in the middle of November was disgraceful but I digress. The whole fiasco brought on a massive migraine and I came so close to cancelling Guernsey. There'd been several times I'd been close to cancelling it, it was just so stressful. I couldn't plan holidays. I hadn't had one for twenty five years up to Center Parcs and Matt and Helena had booked all of that, I couldn't do it, it was all too much. I'd do this then never again. If migraines were going to return I couldn't travel, they left me too weak to sit up or at best leave the house. Couldn't be done.

I wasn't the only one with problems. Earlier in the year a psychic reel had come on Facebook and said make a note of September 5th, so I did, wondering what it could be for, hoping it would be something pleasant. A significant event occurred during that week but it's not my news to record here but I feel it should be mentioned for the family members it related to. All I will say is possibly those involved were being looked after by a higher power, and the outcome was a good one over time.

It wasn't all bad however; we had a big birthday in October, Elliott's 40th, which they'd arranged a meal for family and friends at The Quarter, Potbank, in Stoke, the old Spode works, which was good because the taxi knew exactly where it was and it wasn't too far away for me to get to and back home.

As often happened for me it was touch and go whether I'd make it as I'd hit a rough patch health wise and I was hoping Jesus was good for the impossible asks to get me to it. He was thank goodness and as always I was very grateful. I'd felt better but I'd also felt worse but was just delighted to be there for my boy's special day.

Elliott and Charlotte sat at a table with our family, (Charlotte and Anna being only a year apart in age were inseparable at family get togethers,) Hayley and Harry at the next table with her family, and a third table was next to that for their friends.

The meal was superb, great choice of food which we'd ordered before – I had roast beef and Yorkshire pudding, some of which I brought home, I'm never sure of Yorkshire pudding because of the egg so better to eat it at home with all the facilities!!

All was good and I enjoyed it later for my tea.

Anna had given us a little demo of the dance she'd

performed in her show the previous evening. I hadn't been able to go which I was so disappointed about but I can't manage two outings on consecutive days, I need a rest day – or two – in between. Perhaps next time. I'd seen Charlotte's dance show earlier in the year and she'd performed her two dances well but she wasn't up for giving us a demo just then.

The cake was spectacular; a 40, baked by a friend of theirs and Hayley said later she'd had a hand in the decorating with her. It was wonderful, even with a miniature bottle of Bailey's on it! All in all a great celebration.

The rest of the family went back to Elliott and Hayley's house but my energy wouldn't hold out for that; I was just glad I'd been able to attend the meal. Later they sent me photos of him opening my gifts, memorable, sensible ones and the ubiquitous joke one which was a toilet roll with 40 on it saying, 'I love the (poo emoji) outta ya,' because he's never off the toilet!!! He laughed and said, 'You know me well!'

December brought Matt and family's visit to Center Parcs but I didn't go that time because of saving both money and energy reserves for Guernsey – not to mention that Cadent had robbed me of £700, so I had Rooney.

Shortly after on the 18th was Hayley's birthday and as I sat in bed in the morning I texted her Happy Birthday and asked her if she was doing anything special and she replied that they were going out for tea with her parents and I could join them if I liked, it was only to the carvery down the road from them, Elliott would bring me home if I got a taxi to theirs.

Could I? I felt OK and had washed my hair.

It was so close to Christmas though. I was always bothered about picking up a cold – or Covid although when I believed I'd had that I hadn't been as ill as with a cold which put me in bed for several days – I didn't want to miss Christmas.

What to do? I really wanted to go but dare I?

I don't live my life by tarot cards but I do love them and have found them to be accurate on several occasions, I'd ask them. Should I go, yes or no? The star card. Yes! Happy joyful card. Next card. Would I be OK for Christmas if I did? Queen of Pentacles, another yes and it says that court cards usually apply to the querent so I took it as a good sign so I went and it was a lovely evening even though it lashed it down with rain.

Harry Boy once he'd been settled with Minions or something on YouTube – Shua as he called it in his own special language – was as good as gold although he hadn't decided up until that point if he was going to go along with all of this confined sitting still!

We laughed at Charlotte, out of the mouths of babes and all that. She sometimes had a bit of a thing about dying and she sat opposite Hayley's mum and I, looked at us intently and queried, "Nannar and Nana Shuffs, I wonder who'll die first?"

Elliott and Hayley were aghast and exclaimed, "Charlotte you don't say things like that!"

We nanas meanwhile just laughed.

"It will probably be me," I answered. "I'm the oldest."

Time we went to queue up for our meal!!

Christmas came again, another wonderful one thankfully. I am always thankful to the higher powers who get me to family events which for Christmas for me is my sister Emily's home with her and her family on Christmas Day, and Elliott and Hayley's home on Boxing Day. Always tiring two days together and I need a rest on the 27th but always very grateful to have made it.

Bring on 2025!

Chapter 6

2025

A few years ago a Facebook meme had said, 'Start a whole new life at 70,' and I couldn't wait!

We got New Year's Day off with a party at Matt and Helena's. In the autumn he'd constructed a media wall and sent pictures but I hadn't seen it in the flesh. It was superb. A very professional job housing TV and electric fire with shelf space for ornaments.

I like to think that both my boys have inherited some of my parents creative skills: my dad was a carpenter and my mum used to bake wonderful cakes. Matt had created this wall with such precision and done an excellent job, getting advice on the electrics from Helena's dad who was an electrician; Elliott baked superb cakes for the children's and Hayley's birthdays. We all kept saying he should do Bake Off.

Our February birthdays were Anna's seventh on the

16th, Matt's 44th on the 19th, and my 70th on the 25th. We had a party at Matt and Helena's home for Anna's and Matt's around their birthdays then on Sunday 23rd we'd booked Brindley Farm for a carvery for mine. It had a soft play area for the children so it would keep them entertained especially Harry Boy who didn't like to sit still for too long. Well he was only two years old and it was to be expected!

I didn't tell anyone because I didn't want a cloud to hang over the day but February 23rd 1968 had been the date my mum had died from breast cancer, two days before my 13th birthday, the worst birthday of my life. I was hoping this event was going to wipe those unhappy memories away and replace them with joyful ones.

The weather wasn't great, wind and rain but it didn't matter, we were indoors. I had a taxi and arrived at the same time as everyone else which was good. We were shown to our table which was down the centre of the room alongside the play area. I'd suggested a couple of pictures with the boys and grandchildren at some time during the proceedings so I hoped we could do those. There were balloons on the table with 70 on them and a large helium one in black and gold on a gold ribbon as well which I loved! I'd never had one before!

Lots of lovely gifts from everyone, a large 70 badge, and a beautiful, dainty ring from Elliott and family. It was the first ring I'd ever been given since my wedding ring and that hadn't come in a box but had been a kind of necessity so it was going back a long way and no longer worn following our divorce. It also dispelled the disappointment of a Christmas present many years ago when I thought Barry had got me a ring, saved the small box on my chair as the last present to open, expecting it to be a beautiful sparkling treasure, only to open it and find a box of five After Eight mints!!! He hadn't even bought me a full sized box! 'Well Lovie I don't want you to get fat,' had been his comforting words of consolation as he'd howled with laughter at my disappointment when I'd said, 'Oh, I thought you'd got me a ring.' This little sparkler for my 70th more than made up for that. It was a tiny diamond with two smaller ones either side on a gold band and I would treasure it. I put it on right away. It would only fit my little finger, old fingers, knuckles, extra weight etc and I was, and am, scared of losing it; it's very special and will be left to Charlotte when I pop off.

Throughout the meal Matt was insistent that Barry and I have a photo together.

"No," I said. "We've been divorced for thirty years, we've invited each other to our 70th birthdays, that's quite enough, we'll be on photos with everyone."

Barry had given me a bottle of champagne which I can't really drink alcohol, a thimbleful gives me a terrible headache and said, 'Drink it before you go to Guernsey,' and I said, 'No, it'll make me ill, I'll drink it when I get back, perhaps we can have a small get together and share it.'

Towards the end of the meal Elliott asked the waitress to bring in the cake. I was so thrilled that he'd made me a cake, I'd nursed a tiny hope that he might. It was spectacular! Cream coloured butter icing with gold swirls and a gold 'Happy 70th Birthday' sign stuck in, with candles as well. It had been many years since I'd blown out candles!

"We burned it a bit," Charlotte informed me sitting next to me, "so Dad had to cut it off."

"Charlotte you don't have to tell her that!" added Elliott, and by way of explanation, "*someone*... turned the cooker up; we don't know who!!"

Harry Boy was partial to twiddling knobs and my washing machine knobs were usually on different settings after his visits so he was probably a strong suspect, scuppering his father's expert creation!

We managed to take some good photos with me and the boys and grandchildren, then it was time to leave and pay, or might have paid before, not sure, Matt and Helena paid for my meal. Anyway something was being paid for, we all kind of stood around, Barry and I next to each other, I was just behind, Matt just in front with his phone in his hand. I knew exactly what would happen when he turned round and saw us and it did. He got his photo of us together. Not a bad one of me surprisingly as I was laughing because I knew what he was going to do, a very serious one of Barry because he hadn't seen it coming. 'You could have got me smiling!' he exclaimed. I told Matt what I'd said to my online friend at Center Parcs and she'd said about the Brian Rix farce of adult children throwing their divorced parents together and we laughed.

Elliott and Hayley drove me home with all of my gifts and the remainer of the cake which I'd saved some for Emily and family. Still raining and windy and the balloon ribbon wrapped around my neck as I crossed the car park and I thought I'd be strangled before I got to my actual birthday but all was well. I drove quickly round to Emily's house when I got back to drop their cake off then relaxed when I got back home. Later I got a text from Barry's cousin's wife who we'd always got on well with to say they'd left me some flowers by the front door but I'd been out. It must have been in the few minutes I'd been at Emily's and I'd not noticed when I'd got back. I was very disappointed to miss them; such a lovely thought and we'd always got on so well and it had been years since I'd seen them. We promised to catch up so I hoped we would.

My actual birthday, 25th, I kept free because as was the usual procedure for birthdays, online friends all send wishes to each other in the form of videos etc and lovely and very welcome that they are my head can't take them as well as an outing so I keep family plans for separate days. Thus the usual Tunstall Tea Party, or fish, chips and ice cream at Westport Lake with Emily, Alistair and Cassie, my niece if she wasn't working, had been planned for the 26th. We were very lucky with the weather this time, dry and sunny if a bit of a chilly breeze. We always have a laugh at old memories. Back in our youth, after the letters to my Guernsey date had fizzled out – I'd accepted when I got on the boat to come home that I'd never see him again, the letters had been a bonus, so I knew it could never be, much as I'd have liked otherwise – I decided that the next one to ask me out that was reasonable I'd go. BIG MISTAKE! My dad called him Spineless because he stood me up – twice!

Why I even gave him a second chance I'll never know. Why I even agreed to a second date I'll never know! He wasn't anywhere near in the same league as my Guernsey date but well you have to move on and accept what is don't you, so I went out with the lying creep.

I met him at Tiffany's in Newcastle and agreed to the date; he'd pick me up in his Cortina he said. I waited by C&A in Hanley and he came strutting up Stafford Street – late. Hmm, no Cortina I thought. Figment of his imagination?? First lie. Anyway I won't go into great detail about him, that's covered in Shadow Across the Sun but Emily once double dated with us with his mate. Why we bothered neither of us knew but there you go. During the Tunstall Tea Parties we have a laugh at the horrors of old times which was where most of our dates were and shudder as we drive past the Sneyd Arms, his local. I feel physically sick when I see or think of that establishment.

Emily went into the chip shop in the square opposite said salubrious establishment then Alistair drove to Westport Lake and parked up for us to eat them. Afterwards we got out for a few photos. Emily's not one for photos and forbids any postings on social media in any way, shape or form but she got Cassie to take a few of her and I together. Perhaps it was the sisters thing, 70th birthday that brought out a bit of sentiment. She quipped later as she sent them to me, 'Two old women out for a stroll!' They weren't bad actually. Must have got us on a good day! Perhaps the sun helped! It was a good setting too beside the lake with the stark branches of the trees, not yet showing any spring shoots. Maybe our coats complimented each other, her big coat, cosy cream with a fur edged hood, mine light blue to match the sky that day.

Back to the car and ice cream next. Alistair had said at my last birthday and mentioned it a couple of times after, 'I enjoyed your birthday Shez!' I think we all did! There must have been a light shower somewhere because a beautiful rainbow shone in the distance but we hadn't noticed rain, it must have been brief. Then the presents.

Gifts are always lovely both to give and receive. I always think the sentiment and that our loved ones have thought about us, whether friends or family, adds towards the meaning of them and this 70th birthday had extra special meaning.

Emily brought them all in from the boot of the car. Firstly a balloon in the shape of a two tier birthday cake, then gift bags of goodies from all of them which consisted of a lovely fleece throw and reed diffuser from Cassie, seeds for the garden, a unicorn money box, bath goodies and a lovely Sister 70th keyring from Emily and Alister, plus the kind of joke present.

It was a purple sash which I expected to say Happy 70th Birthday on it but instead it said, 'WHAT NOW.' I gasped and howled with laughter. My every day saying, several times a day in the kitchen or wherever because I can't remember what I've gone in there for!!! So funny. She said she'd asked if she could have it when she'd ordered it and the woman said you can have whatever you like.

I also had another 70 badge from Cassie. All lovely gifts from family and friends. I'd been very spoiled.

My 13th birthday when Mum had died had been my worst birthday ever; this one, my 70th, had been my absolute best!

Chapter 7

We were all starting to talk about Guernsey more each time we met up. Charlotte kept saying to me, 'I'm going to Guernsey with Anna, are you coming?' and I'd say, 'yes, it's part of my 70th birthday celebrations.'

I'd also arranged another visit to Center Parcs for December with Matt and family which I was looking forward to. Two holidays in a year! I'd never done that in my entire life!! 2025 was looking great so far.

It was during 2024 though that I'd had the idea for the two books with a Guernsey theme: this one, and I'd decided to set my Willows Dip Book Eight partly in Guernsey. I was hoping for both to get a proper feel of the island when we were visiting to give authenticity to the novel, and this memoir would be a record of the holiday.

I'd already had characters go on holiday to Guernsey in Book Five, Not Reported Missing, never dreaming as I wrote that I'd ever go again, but I thought I'd have something a bit more permanent with new characters. I asked in two Guernsey Facebook groups, Guernsey Days Gone By and Guernsey in the Old Days, if people retired to Guernsey from the UK and apart from a few quips of only if they've won Euromillions, many people were very helpful, posting links, some suggesting inheriting a property, marrying a local, also explaining their two tier property system which sounded so complex to me. It all gave me plenty to think about. I also wanted to incorporate a scene from Liberation Day 1945 for a character, which again people were very helpful with, sharing their family memories, some of them really moving.

I'd got a young police officer and his family in my Willows Dip series but I'd decided his father, a retired dog handler, could be my main character, so it all went from there. I put another post in the group asking about the crime rate in Guernsey and dog handlers and once again lots of lovely people responded with helpful answers.

More help came from an author friend, a retired detective from Staffordshire police, John Pye, who answered my police questions from this end so lots of kindness in helping me with my research. John's books are superb crime stories with tremendous attention to detail. The first I read was Where the Silent Screams are Loudest, which went on to win The Arnold Bennett Book Prize. Very well deserved. I also read all of his 'Of Lies' series. Excellent crime stories with the authenticity of someone who knows first hand of police investigations. I don't normally read crime, too scared, but I read his as

I knew him from a local literary event which ran monthly before covid lockdown, 6x6 Reading Café, and enjoyed the stories he read out. His books are all available on Amazon. As I write this I'm reading his current novel Pray to the Devils, excellent!

Something that made me ask for more help both from John and Guernsey was a review I had for Not Reported Missing in which she said she'd have liked to have known more about the policeman. This was a different policeman but I knew I needed to get deeper under his skin, into his head, see what made him tick and who better to ask than those who had been in the job?!

Two family events in March were Charlotte's 6th birthday party and Anna's dance show. I was hoping to be well for both because I'd missed both the previous ones: Charlotte's 5th birthday because I'd unwittingly watched a fast moving video reel on Facebook for all of a few seconds and it had triggered a migraine that had lasted for two weeks, and Anna's show because it was the evening before Elliott's 40th birthday meal and I couldn't do two events together.

First up was Charlotte's birthday and I was delighted to make it! The obvious reason being her birthday but there was also a new family member in the shape of Hayley's brother and partner's almost three month old baby daughter. Always lovely to welcome a new baby and Charlotte was delighted that her newest cousin was there at her party. It helped dim the disappointment that her other cousins were unable to make it; all of Matt's family had something going on that couldn't be changed.

Christian had been signed recently by a semi professional football club, Whitchurch Alport, and had a game, Anna had her last show rehearsal and Rosie had gone down with a stomach bug. All was not lost though, they had a party the next day for school friends at a soft play park that they were going to, not Christian, he was too old at sixteen unless just to be there, so Charlotte got her cousin time. Barry was also away so it was just me from our family but it was a lovely occasion as we all always got on well as a whole family.

The cake, Elliott's creation, was remarked on by all. Spectacular as ever. Tall, rainbow coloured, sponge and butter icing coating, with the swirls he'd done on my 70th cake. "Wait until you see inside," he told us, excited to get our reaction. We all thought at first it was the rainbow colours to the layers as he cut into it, but they were like doughnut shaped and the whole of the centre was filled with Haribo sweets and Smarties. Charlotte gasped in delight and everyone else gasped in wonder at his culinary skills. It tasted as delicious as it looked and I was so thankful to be well off the evil metformin diabetic drug which had made me so sick and unable to tolerate anything remotely sweet. Far better to control it by diet and have a treat now and then. It was a wonderful party and as with any occasion I was delighted to have been able to join in.

The next event was Anna's show and again I was relived to be well enough to attend. Matt said as Anna was already at the theatre they'd have room for me in the car so they'd pick me up but I'd need to get a taxi back as they'd all go straight home after the show. That was great, no problem to get a taxi, the theatre was only in town, a ten minute drive away.

We were driving off the estate where I live and towards town when he said, "Guess who's pregnant."

"Who?"

"Helena!"

I was amazed! "What now?" I asked. Stupid question. My usual saying but different context!

She smiled from the passenger seat. "Yes."

"That's lovely! Was it a surprise?"

"No it was planned, it just happened sooner than we expected."

"How far?"

"I'm about seven weeks."

"That's lovely!" I turned to Rosie and Christian beside me. "What do you think?"

They were both excited and had been thinking about names.

"Anna was a bit upset," Matt said, "she won't be the youngest anymore."

"It's a real surprise. How lovely."

"Yes, so when we go to Center Parcs in December we'll have a really young baby," declared Helena.

"Yes it'll certainly be exciting won't it."

We'd arrived at the theatre by then and Matt parked behind the building and we met Helena's parents and Barry and went inside. He was as surprised as I was and her parents had been the night before when they'd told them. A new family member. How wonderful! Something else for 2025.

The show was a mix of Wicked and The Wizard of Oz, which I knew the story of but I didn't know the story of Wicked so that was new to me. Very good though and Anna performed her dances well. She was Ruby Red-stone, a little red ladybird and very pretty with her long blonde hair. The taxi arrived almost as soon as I rang for it once the show was over and we got outside into the sunshine, a lovely spring day, a fabulous show and wonderful family news. What could be better!

Chapter 8

Easter Sunday was a lovely sunny day if a little cool, and I'd been invited to Helena's parents for lunch with them all which was lovely. Her mum was an excellent cook and I love a roast dinner; she did lamb being Easter with raspberry cheesecake or lemon meringue pie for dessert. I used to love lemon meringue pie but it was another item on the no list for the contrary insides both for the lemon and egg whites but it looked gorgeous and was Matt and Barry's favourite. I chose the cheesecake which was delicious. We ate in the conservatory which her dad had constructed himself and done an amazing job on. I wouldn't have the first idea of where to start.

I left at three thirty to be back home in time for the dogs, Rooney and Ralph to be dropped off for a week's stay at Nana Shuffs dog hotel whilst their families were away: Elliott and family were going to a Haven site in Great Yarmouth, Matt and family to Center Parcs, their special place. The men arrived with the dogs at six and after an initial greeting which we guided them outside, they settled down, well kind of, they like to go round the garden and mark their spots – the dogs that is not the lads!! They sat and had a beer and we had a pleasant chat. When they left with handshakes and wishing each other a good holiday and kisses for me the dogs were eager for the more serious business of opening the treat boxes; they love those little gravy bones and for bigger treats they have a Bonio biscuit or a stick. All are enjoyed equally.

The fun part came at bedtime, well perhaps confusion is a more appropriate description. The routine goes thus. Outside for last wee, I gather my drinks in bottles for during the night and my last and first thing cuppa which I make upstairs, saves trudging up and down, much more convenient, in my Little Red Riding Hood basket and up the stairs we go. They know this procedure well and are up the stairs way before me even though both have a touch of arthritis as do I. They are very patient whilst I'm making the tea, going to the loo etc and they are waiting for their two gravy bones secreted away in the basket, then as I sit in bed, they have their biscuits and I let them on for an hour while I have my tea and ginger biscuit, not a lot of room left with me and two labradoodles, good job I haven't got a significant other! Poor man would be battling for space!

They have to get off when I go to sleep, I can't have movement on the bed, they have their own beds, Roon's at the left side of my bed, Ralph's at the right. Ralph gets off of his own accord after about half an hour and gets settled on his own bed. Not so Roon, he's very comfy and dead to the world on mine thank you very much. I need a last toilet visit before sleep so he has to get off. Here it goes.

"Come on Roon off you get."

No movement.

"Roon, on your bed."

Nothing.

A more firm, "On your bed!"

Doesn't budge.

"Roon! On your bed!!" Lifts his head and looks at me befuddled.

Meanwhile I became aware of Ralph wandering round equally bemused. Off his bed. On his bed. Off his bed. On Roon's bed. Poor boy didn't know whether he was coming or going with this command of 'On your bed!' As far as he was concerned he was on his!

Me, I was getting a mite frustrated being more than a little tired after a busy day. "No not you, you go on your own bed!"

Poor Ralph hung his head as if to say well I was on it and nice and comfy thank you very much until you started barking orders. Roon looked at me hopefully and I said ,'No, off,' pointing to his bed and he obeyed if rather truculently. It did make me laugh though. Poor Ralph had been completely bewildered.

The following night I had to haul Roon off physically so I decided no to getting on at night, I was too tired for that, they could just get on in the morning when they would both get off ready for breakfast.

On Monday morning I thought we'd have a little fun. We did one of my 'A sherry with Sherrie' videos for my book promotions. To steal the words of a friend I employed actors, my two furry thespians to promote the two books they featured in, My Furry Loves, an animal memoir about all of the pets I've had throughout life, and Sonnets, a collection of sonnets, one of which is about the trial run we had to see if I could manage to have them together.

I got my table out and my sherry in one of my new glasses, my little treasures I'd treated myself to from EBay, once someone else's treasures but now mine; I'd loved them as soon as I'd seen them, gold stemmed with a rose on them, their first outing on this video. A Bonio for the dogs was a necessity along with a couple of gravy bones lined up waiting to keep them on hand for the end of the show. They performed perfectly if wondering what all of this rigmarole was about and why I'd taken leave of my senses and begun talking to myself sipping from a glass. In fact they did so well we did another one in the garden later in the week in the sunshine and sat out for a while, which we all seemed to enjoy. I think if doggy film awards were given out they'd certainly be deserving of one. As it was they got 300+ views and 25 likes on Tik Tok and loads of responses from friends on Facebook.

The week went well aside from a hiccup health wise for me but they were so good while I spent an extra hour lying on my bed; Ralph won't come up during the day so he stayed downstairs on his bed, although when I went down he was sitting in the lounge doorway as if to say, 'Where's me dinner?' Roon is always up for a lie on the bed so he came up with me.

The end of the week arrived and Elliott came for Ralph and Matt and Helena for Roon. They'd all had a good time and I was happy to be able to have the dogs so that they could go and make memories. I always love to see their delight when their families come to collect them. They're happy enough with me and love the treats and a lie on the bed but it's not their home and they are delighted to see their families and jump in the car to leave Nana Shuffs dog hotel. For me I quite enjoy having them together, see how they interact. The downside is twice the poo lifting which is a killer on the old back and when I let them out with a groan and say 'Come on then let's see if you've got anymore,' they just wag their tails delightedly whilst I stand there with a look of resignation! Then starts the general clean up once they've gone.

Chapter 9

The next event, well double event was Rosie's 11th birthday combined with gender reveal party at Matt and Helena's home on a June Saturday. As with all events I look forward to them, hoping my health conditions don't have any party tricks of their own – they did. The return of the dreaded migraines for simply looking at a very short video on Facebook at the beginning of the week, added to by taking paracetamol extra pills that contained caffeine, which made them worse, by Friday it didn't look as though I'd be fit to attend. However I did have a trick of my own up my sleeve, a magic zopiclone sleeping pill kept for special events to damp down the nervous system and Saturday morning it all looked more promising. Of course I needed a little whisper in Jesus' ear to ask the impossible! I was going!

The twenty minute taxi journey was uneventful but my head, dancing to its own tune didn't like the noise of the traffic nor the visual movement, too much sensory overload and by the time I arrived at Matt's house I was feeling like hell, stomach turning somersaults and I just slumped on the settee. I asked Anna to get me a drink of water whilst I watched Rosie open her presents beneath the spectacular display of black and gold balloons and stars around the media wall, and she told me about her birthday. It took an hour or more to feel slightly better but I was just glad I was able to be there for the celebrations.

It was a big party with their friends and neighbours as well as family and the weather was very kind to us. Although in the middle of a heatwave it had started off cloudy but the promised sun had come out around lunchtime and it was a glorious day, just right for all outdoor activities. There was a bouncy castle for the children and also the pool was out for them all to swim in. The 'Girl or Boy' display with lots of blue and pink balloons stood beside the bouncy castle waiting for the reveal later. Rosie's friends arrived and she had lots more presents, several cuddly toys which she loved, books, clothes, craft activities; she did very well.

Everyone had a wonderful time, great food, barbeque, sandwiches, fresh fruit and so much more, too much to mention, cakes of course and a superb birthday cake. Then came the reveal. On the wall in the kitchen by the open patio doors was a chart and we'd all been adding our votes as to what we thought the baby was, boy or girl by adding a blue baby vest to one side or a pink to the other and putting our name on. The blues were winning but would we be right?

The three children, Christian, Rosie and Anna each had a tube, cannon I think they were called to hold in their hand and pull, like a large party popper and blue or pink confetti would erupt. They took their places out on the lawn in front of the bouncy castle beside the 'Girl or Boy' display and Christian went first to pull. Pink or Blue?

Bang! Pink and white confetti erupted into the air. A girl!

"Three daughters!" exclaimed Helena.

The girls pulled theirs and more confetti danced on the air against the backdrop of blue sky and settled on the grass. Everyone cheered and chatted at once. Christian looked stunned.

"Three sisters," I said to him, among the many other comments and he grinned.

Everyone digested the news and talked all at once. I'd had a feeling it would be a boy but I was wrong. Another granddaughter would be lovely, and something to look forward to in the autumn. Time for me to leave. I'd done well under the influence of a lingering migraine but was so pleased to have been a part of it all. The party went on long into the evening and Rosie had some of her friends to sleep over.

We had one more party before Guernsey and that would be Harry's third birthday but I would have to miss that one because it would be the weekend before we went and I would need to pace myself for the holiday, plus I didn't want to risk picking up any form of germs from the taxi, you never knew who'd been in them before you!

Chapter 10

Wednesday 6th August 2025
Guernsey!

For the last few weeks I'd fluctuated between excitement and flutters of panic. What was I doing? What was I thinking? I was seventy, lived alone, never flown, never left the UK since Guernsey when I was nineteen, young and healthy, able to get around and do what I wanted. Now here I was embarking on this hairbrained idea with a restrictive health condition. All of my lovely online M.E friends in the Facebook group had been so supportive and encouraging. It had been some of them who'd advised wheelchair assistance at the airports because of the walking and standing in queues, even though I don't normally use one, some of them even went on holiday alone – very brave – but all said it could be done with careful planning and even the payback of falling into an M.E crash of exhaustion –

P.E.M (post exertional malaise) – when they got home, was worth it for the experience, so I was going.

I sat waiting for the taxi, Steve's Travel, sourced from Facebook recommendations; his brother Brian was picking me up bound for Manchester airport at 11 a.m. He arrived on time; both he and Steve had texted me the day before so I was reassured they would be here. The airline Aurigny (pronounced areeny) had also been in touch a few days before as had Milton Travel agents who'd booked my flights and my boarding pass was through, all new to me having never flown before; everyone had done a wonderful job in making my journey as smooth as possible.

Brian was very pleasant, collecting my case and carry on bag from the door, easy to talk to; the minibus was lovely and clean and comfortable. I locked up and said goodbye and be safe to my little house and we set off.

Brian was very chatty and I told him it was my first flight at the old age of seventy and he said I'd love it – I did! As we approached the airport he showed me a little lane where he said he'd wait for me when he picked me up and to text him when I'd got my luggage and he'd be there when I came out.

It all seemed huge. It had been many years since I'd been to Manchester airport to take and pick up Emily and Alistair, my sister and brother in law from their honeymoon in 1983 and it only had one terminal at that time. Matt then aged two and I had watched their plane take off for Corfu from the window. It was completely different now. Brian showed me where to go but couldn't wait so I went inside to look around to see if the family were already there. It was huge and so many people. I can't begin to describe it because it was all so new to me I didn't know what was what and where the check in desks were or anything, it just seemed a jumble of people all milling round dragging suitcases like an army of ants dragging their leaves. At this point a fleeting thought flashed that I was thankful for Sara's diet that had also balanced brain chemicals that controlled anxiety because previously I'd have been off my head with it. I was also thankful that the migraines of the previous few weeks had cleared because I couldn't let myself think how I'd have coped if they hadn't. I went back outside and there was Elliott and family just walking up towards the entrance, I spotted Charlotte first, pulling her red carry on bag.

We'd had one major disappointment. Matt and family had had to cancel. Helena had suffered from a herniated disc since early in her pregnancy and was in constant pain and had been advised by her doctors not to leave the UK. We were all immensely disappointed, we had all been looking forward to the family being together; it had been Matt's idea from the outset, Helena had looked forward to it from when we'd discussed it at Center Parcs and she'd said, 'We'll go anywhere,' but these things happen and can't be helped. We would miss them terribly. There would be a Wobble (family nickname) sized hole in our holiday.

We all met up, I was very relieved to see them so soon, and Elliott took their car keys to whichever desk he had to, they always did it when they went away but it seemed very trusting to me, I don't think I'd want to hand my car keys over but perhaps that's just me being old, then we made our way to the disabled area just inside the door that I'd seen earlier. I gave my name to the lady on the desk and by some kind of magic created by the travel agents and airline it was there! She said to take a seat and I asked could my family come in as well, she asked were they happy to push me, yes, so we found a seat and settled ourselves for a snack. Time soon passed then we went to the check in desk where Hayley checked us in and Elliott pushed me in the wheelchair, it felt very strange, my son whom I'd pushed in the pram and buggy now pushing me. Quite dependent but I couldn't have managed that amount of walking or standing. The children were very good whilst we waited. Then came the fun bit; security.

All of this was new to me so I just went along with all the herding and did what Elliott said. When we got to the whatever the thing was, conveyor belt, he told me to take my watch off, cardi, etc and put them in the tray, they went through the scanner whilst we went round to the human scanner; Hayley went through with the children. There was quite a queue as being August summer holidays it was busy, Elliott said later it wasn't normally that busy when they'd been. This was where the fun began.

Elliott got scanned no problem. My turn. The woman asked could I stand. Yes. I stood in the scanner spot and everything lit up! Bits of me that had no business lighting up! Why?? Shoes had to come off. Feet scanned. Everything scanned with the hand held body scanner. Thoroughly frisked! The lot!!! Baptism of fire! I had visions of being whisked off to some room and being strip searched! "Move your feet further apart," demanded the grim faced young woman. Scanned again. "Sit down." She didn't even say if it was OK. Was I to wait for further instructions? I was reassured minimally to see another younger woman get similar treatment and I said to Elliott, "Are we OK to go?" so he asked her and received a curt nod.

We looked at each other with a grin. "It lit up your personal bits," he pointed out.

"I know! What do they expect to find?? It's been many a long year since anything has gone on down there!"

He recoiled with a horrified laugh. "NO! DON'T! I don't want to know!" Then he laughed properly. "I can't wait to tell Matt."

We both laughed, me from my exalted position in the pushchair. "Let's go and find Hayley," he continued.

We laughed when we told her our experience but she'd had the same with the children, both of them had to have their shoes taken off and soles of their feet scanned. Whatever they thought young children and old women were trafficking on the soles of their feet we had no idea but all done we progressed on to the better part of snacks.

Again I had no idea what was going on and couldn't hear what was being said over the speaker system and couldn't see the screen but Hayley kept checking. It was only after we got home that they said we'd come close to missing the flight because it hadn't announced boarding on the screen and they'd just heard final call so it had been a rush through the lifts whilst trying not to alarm me. I had no clue. Nor did it register that we were the last to get on the shuttle bus to get out to the aircraft on the tarmac.

It seemed a long drive out to where the lovely little yellow and white Aurigny plane with its red, gold and white Guernsey flag on it waited for us. Hayley looked a mite nervous as she took a couple of photos of it. "I've never been on such a small plane!" she exclaimed. "I'm used to not looking at them and just getting on." Nonetheless we all boarded and that was where the next hitch came.

I should have been in seat 4A behind them but somewhere along the line I ended up right down the back in seat 16, miles away from them; a bit daunting for a first flight but at least I was on it so I was glad of that. The flight attendant showed me to my seat next to a younger woman who I'd seen earlier checking her family in, and carried on with her business. The woman next to me was very friendly, we exchanged names later in the journey, she was Karen and they were going to Guernsey for her mum's ninetieth birthday at the end of August, they'd been to Jersey for her dad's the year before. I said our trip was part of my seventieth birthday celebrations and it was my first flight.

"Oh I'll swap seats with you," she offered, "so you can see through the window," which was lovely of her. We didn't do it until after take off though and a little way into the flight.

We had a laugh about various topics and her family joined in, the two men in front of us, and the man and woman opposite the aisle to them and her parents in front of them; lovely people. I loved the flight, being up above the clouds and in between them seeing the fields below. When we got over the channel the boats and the wash behind them sparkled in the sunlight looking so tiny like toys.

"Ooh we're over islands!" I exclaimed. "We must be nearly there."

I took several photos and two of the islands I learned from the Guernsey Days Gone By Facebook group later were Brechqou, owned by the Barclay Brothers who owned the Telegraph newspaper, and Little Sark. I like to know my whereabouts.

"Let me take your photo," Karen said, so I did to record my first flight.

"Do you want another with your boyfriend?" offered the man in front.

"Ooh I've pulled on the plane!" I replied and Karen laughed. "She says she's pulled on the plane," she told him.

"Is he your husband?" I asked her.

"My brother. My husband is opposite."

We all laughed, then I think the pilot announced that we were starting our descent and to fasten our seatbelts. All very exciting. We were in Guernsey where I hadn't been since I was a teen!

Again the airport assistance was superb and wheelchairs were waiting at the bottom of the steps of the aircraft for Karen's father and I, he couldn't walk too far either. Always someone carried my bag which was lovely. Everyone had been very helpful; everything very well organized. We went straight out into the arrival lounge, Elliott, Hayley and the children got the luggage. The hire car department was right there in the building so that was easily done, child seats were fitted and we could go.

The next hitch; I wouldn't fit in the car with the child seats. Although it was a five seater there wasn't enough room so it meant getting a taxi which wasn't a problem as they were there waiting at the airport; the problems came later getting back from wherever we'd been.

It was a kind of surreal feeling to be back after all these years. Familiar and yet not. Albany Apartments looked wonderful but I couldn't relate them to the disco in Birnam Court hotel as it had been back in the 70s. I'd thought the road had been flatter where it's actually on a hill, but we were young and fit and walked everywhere so we probably hadn't noticed that. I'd remembered it as being further back from the road but perhaps that's my memory wrong again. I didn't know what alterations it had undergone from hotel to apartments or when. Debbie was waiting to greet us when we arrived and show us to our apartments. Charlotte is very chatty and informed her that we were here for Nana Shuffs birthday and her brother's birthday. From there we parted company and settled in.

My apartment was number three, just like my house at home, in a very pretty little courtyard. Debbie unlocked the door, showed me around the rooms and left me to settle in. It was lovely, comfortable sitting room and bedroom overlooking the gardens, each with a patio door opening onto them, en suite to the bedroom and the kitchen was off the sitting/dining room. A lovely home from home. I was to find out later that the bed was the comfiest ever and so were the pillows, even for my funny neck! Hayley had booked an online grocery shop which was delivered later and she brought mine down to me then Elliott called down later to check I was OK before we all settled for the night and to have a look at my apartment. He said they were very pleased with their's and I'd made a good choice sourcing them. My little courtyard was all lit up with white and blue lights round the steps, so pretty.

My sleep patterns aren't great and I managed about four hours, broken! I was up, showered and hair washed by seven. Well I say up, dressed etc but resting on the bed. Elliott came over around eight thirty for a coffee and we chatted about our first night; they'd all slept well, children as well. They were going to go in the pool later but he asked if there was anything I wanted to do and I said I'd like to get some postcards if we could have a look for some and I wouldn't mind a quick drive through St Peter Port just for a look. This materialized faster than I expected because Harry Boy had a sleep so Elliott came for me and we made a dash out.

He was getting used to the hire car; it was automatic where his own was manual, also the twisty roads were a bit of a challenge. They live very close to a dual carriage-way so most of their journeys involve that so Guernsey's smaller roads were very different. For myself I'd prefer smaller roads, my dual carriageway driving days are long gone, my days of a bit of speed beating people off at the lights in my lovely little XR3i belonging to my forties. Anyway I thought he was doing pretty well and I recognised some places from YouTube.

I wanted a then and now photo from when I was here before when I was nineteen. I'd been standing by a wall by the marina but where exactly it was I'd no idea. As I've mentioned we walked everywhere when we were young and just took photos wherever we were so I didn't know where to look but we found somewhere by a wall with Herm and Jethou in the background, not the exact spot but it would suffice. We drove around looking for little shops with postcard stands but couldn't see any and somehow ended up in Waitrose. The closest one to me at home is Leek, Staffordshire. Never been in but always been curious as to how more affluent shoppers live so we had a look but no they didn't sell postcards. We got milk though, lovely creamy Guernsey milk, and yoghurt for me – oh and a bag! I'd use it to go to the shop at home to look proper posh! No postcards but Elliott said they'd have a look if they went out later.

Some of the afternoon was spent by the pool. The sun was trying its best to come out and Elliott and Charlotte had braved it and gone in. Charlotte was like a little fish! I'd never mastered swimming underwater but she was brilliant! Harry wasn't quite sure and he and Hayley just had a paddle on the steps; I'd have a dabble another day. Later on they went into St Peter Port and texted did I want to go to them but I was too tired then having only four hours sleep so I didn't, we were planning to go to Oatlands Village the next day so I wanted to be OK for that. They'd got my postcards and stamps though so that was good.

Day 2
Friday 8th August
Oatlands Village

All set for a good card bashing today in Rebecca's Chocolates that I'd seen online, and in the gift shop. I'd made a list, well as far as you can for gifts for people, you have to look don't you.

"See if you can still get Guernsey toms," Emily had said. "We could save the seeds and grow our own." Her first Saturday job had been in Hanley market on the greengrocer's stall and they'd sold Guernsey toms, where I'd first seen them shopping with my mum when I was a child.

"I don't think they grow them commercially now," I told her, "but I'll keep a look out."

We set off, Elliott, Hayley and the children went ahead whilst I waited for the taxi and we met up there. We had a lovely lunch at The Kiln. I only had a cheese sandwich and chips – gorgeous chips! I took half of the sandwich back for my tea, always do wherever I go, I don't eat much, I should be stick thin but sadly I'm not! After that off for a good spend. Ooh I was so looking forward to this, I'd transferred money into my holiday account specially for the purpose. Got a good selection of the delicious delicacies on display, lined them up on the desk – I could have had more, it was just like Charlie and the Chocolate Factory but I managed to rein myself in, got to the till, confidently brandished said card for bashing – declined!!! What!! There's plenty in there and I'd just paid the taxi? Had he robbed me?

"Put your card in and try with your pin," the very nice lady suggested.

No, the card machine was having none. Never let it be said I'm one to panic but I had visions of the whole account being cleaned out. I wasn't too worried about paying as I'd taken cash but what was worrying was what had happened to the account. My heart sank at the thought of a phone call to the bank when I got back to the apartment which would completely blag my head. I'd try it at the gift shop and see if it was just a glitch.

No, no luck at the gift shop either but among the many delightful gifts I managed to get Emily's Guernsey tom, a cuddly one, not one with seeds, and a Guernsey notebook gift to self. You can never have too many notebooks can you, well I can't and I've got my notes in it now as I type.

Elliott and Hayley stayed later and took the children to the play barn and I had a twenty minute wait for the taxi which did nothing to sweeten my mood. However he was a lovely man, very chatty and we tried my card yet again but no luck, my cash now had a big hole in it. He gave me change in Guernsey money which I was pleased with.

"Ooh I'll save this," I told him, "I didn't last time. I've been here before when I was nineteen."

"I thought you looked familiar," he replied and we laughed. "Guernsey money won't be any use to you anywhere else."

"No I know, I just want to save it."

I also asked him about booking a taxi to take me to the airport and he suggested booking it sooner rather than later to be on the safe side. We'd only need to be there an hour before check in. What a change from three hours at Manchester!

I checked my phone when I got back and there was a text from the bank. Suspicious activity on your card, suspected fraud at Rebecca's Chocolates. Was this you? Yes, No, option. Yes! Thank you for responding. Try your card in five minutes, or words to that effect. Well at least that was sorted without a phone call. My poor brain was tired though and needed a massage. Elliott and the children came across later to see if I'd got it sorted and Charlotte had a look in my bags on the coffee table.

"Oh those chocolates look nice," she said wistfully. "Who are they for?"

"Oh, just some of my friends who helped me to book the flight."

"Oh." She closed the bag.

I didn't tell her I'd got some for their family for helping me, it would be a surprise. They trotted off outside with Elliott and I went and had a rest on my bed and watched them through the window as they played What Time Is It Mr Wolf, in the garden. One of my special memories of the holiday.

Day 3
Saturday 9th August
Rest Day

Awake at 3 a.m! Definitely a rest day! I had told myself before we came I must be sure to have rest days.

Generally I can't do something, outings etc two days together, I need rest and recovery in between so holidays will be no different; I'd found this to my cost at Center Parcs when I'd pushed myself to do too much, made myself ill and wanted to come home half way through. I didn't want to make that mistake again either for any further visits there or here, I'd wanted to come back for so long, spent too much money to want to go home, so better to rest.

I did go over to the pool to Elliott and family and went in up to my knees but as for testing if my swimming ability was still intact after my disastrous attempt at Center Parcs, that wasn't happening. I sat at the side in the sun for a while then went back indoors.

Hayley had a meeting with a business colleague who lived in Guernsey and I caught up on my online chats with friends and family.

As I rested on the bed looking through the window it was lovely to watch the fronds of the palm tree swaying in the breeze in the lovely sunshine, see the birds going about their daily lives; there was a family of sparrows that lived in the large shrub to the right of my patio doors and they shared it with a blackbird and either his mate or youngster.

I wondered what they made of all these strangers invading their space but it didn't seem to bother them.

I also made notes in my new Guernsey notebook for my novel, Willows Dip Book Eight which I'm going to call Nancy's Dream, set partly in my usual setting of Willows Dip, a fictional Staffordshire village, and partly in Guernsey, the inspiration being this holiday. I'd asked in the two Guernsey Facebook groups a couple of years ago, Guernsey Days Gone By, and Guernsey in the Old Days, if people from the UK retired to Guernsey and suggestions came up of inheriting a property or marrying a local so I'd thought of an inheritance theme, whether the marriage theme will come in I don't know, I'll see how the story evolves. I made notes on the buildings backing onto the apartments for my descriptions and I hoped to find something I could take a photo of to use as a book cover but I'd have to be careful because you can't go photographing people's property to use without their permission. I'd see what I could come up with.

In the afternoon Elliott and family went into St Peter Port and said did I want to meet them but I hadn't got the energy having been awake since three. I was more than a little jealous because that was where I really wanted to be to retrace old steps so I made the decision to have a sleeping pill in the hope of a decent sleep and go there myself the next day regardless of whether I needed a taxi of not!

We did have some delicious fish and chips that Hayley went out for whilst Elliott watched Arsenal. As I got a plate out of the cupboard I turned it over, a Stokie habit that people from the Potteries do to see where pots are made and sure enough it was made in Hanley, Stoke-on-Trent, a reminder of home.

Day 4
Sunday 10th August
St Peter Port

Success! Slept until 4.12 a.m. seemed to be a bit of a norm, not ideal but it'd do. The sun eventually came out for my visit to St Peter Port and my trip down memory lane, lots of time spent there in 1974 so with the perfect weather it promised to be a good day. As soon as it came light and after my first cuppa and ginger biscuit to kick start the system I texted Elliott and told him of my plans and he said he'd run me into town then I could get a taxi back as they were going in the pool. That was fab, just a taxi one way. I wanted dropping off by Castle Cornet and they'd had a look to see whether they'd want to go but it was a bit expensive on top of other activities they wanted to do so decided against it. I didn't mind going on my own, I had lots to think about. I wanted to relive my memories of where I'd walked with my friends and my date in 1974.

I'll call my date Sam as I did in Shadow Across the Sun, it makes it easier than just saying 'my date.' He'd said on the night we'd met at the disco in Birnam Court Hotel – now Albany Apartments where I was staying – "I could pick you up one night and show you around the island." We went with his friend and mine and I thought this was what Guernsey boys did, showed visiting girls round the island but nonetheless it was special to me and made my holiday magical, and he was lovely.

They took us to a pub where I'm ashamed to say I asked for a vodka and lime – that was two out of his week's pay counting the one on the night we'd met. Looking back I wished I'd asked for a half of shandy, he might have taken me on a second date then – or I'd have been happy with just an ice cream, but I digress, I can't remember the name of the pub or where it was, I'd like to have seen it now if it's still there. All I remember is it had a car park and inside it had fish nets hanging from the ceiling. As we sat on bar stools Sam said something really funny and he, I and the barman all laughed but I can't for the life of me remember what it was and I'd love to! Then we went to Castle Cornet. This is where I wanted to take photos of.

I got Elliott to drop me off there and walked to the beginning of the walkway but it didn't look anything like I remembered. I'd seen pictures in Facebook groups and YouTube and I thought once I got there it would seem more familiar, but it didn't.

To my thoughts when I'd been with Sam he'd just parked the car, we'd got out and walked in a straight line, but maybe it's all changed in fifty one years. I couldn't walk to the castle now, too far, and I couldn't see it very well from where I stood, but I took a few pictures for the memories.

One overriding memory of that balmy summer evening all those years ago was walking back to his car and an overwhelming wave of sadness washing over me as I realized I'd never see him again. I never wanted to leave. I wished I'd met him at home but he wouldn't have been who he was.

Perhaps I was just one of many girls he showed round the island and it was a regular thing to him. I thought this at the end of my holiday as I got on the boat to leave, but for me it was magical, something that has never been repeated, so I'll always thank him for being a special part of a special holiday – that and the vodka!

I can't drink now, only water, so I'm a cheap date, unless I push the boat out and have a J2O.

As I said earlier, we did write for a while. He sent a letter and a photo with his friend to my friend, who'd exchanged addresses, and it was lovely to prolong our… whatever it was. You couldn't call it a relationship, but I always looked forward to his letters.

My dad would sometimes get to the mail before me and say with a twinkle in his eye, "Letter for you from Guernsey." We were young though and far apart geographically, no Internet, WhatsApp or texts back then, and as the autumn leaves began to fall so did our communication.

I still didn't know if it was just a bit of fun for him and a holiday romance for me, but I really liked him, more than anyone I'd ever met.

Ah memories…

I spent a few moments looking over the sea beyond the wall at the boats – I still couldn't believe I was by the sea when I'd thought that I'd never see it again, and never in a million years in Guernsey – then moved onto the marina with all the boats moored, the pellucid blue skies reflected in the water and the pastel coloured bunting on the railings fluttering gently in the slight breeze.

I wondered if there was anywhere to sit down, I can't stand for long or walk far, then saw seats at the bus terminal so walked over there, sat a while, took more photos, then had a walk along the road and found a little tuck shop with post cards.

I wanted some more just for myself, I also needed some more stamps, and to test the flaming debit card!! Thankfully it worked so I did have financial freedom on that score.

I asked the lady in the shop if there was a post box and she said next to the pub so I thought I'd try a wander over there. It was lovely with another rest on a seat in between.

I now came to recognize places I'd seen online: The Town Church, The Albion House Tavern, Victor Hugo's bench. I sat there and did a selfie which was hideous, definitely not one for Facebook ha ha!

After that I sat on the bench behind and just sat, soaking up the atmosphere and the lovely sunshine surrounded by beautiful flowers of red, gold, pink, and thinking I've waited fifty one years for this. I didn't want to move, knowing I probably wouldn't come back but knowing I'd have to go soon. I'm on an energy budget and I'd have to wait for the taxi, so it was with reluctance that I called Island Taxis.

She said to wait by Sports Direct just behind the pub because that was where they waited, and I'm so glad she did because I got to look at the pretty streets with more coloured bunting and beautiful buildings, and get a few photos. I couldn't walk there now, too steep, too far for me, but lovely to see, and I spied Guernsey Gifts and nipped in quickly thinking the taxi would be a while as it had coming from Oatlands.

But no, it arrived in the ten minutes she'd said.

I did have time to grab three gifts to self though: a bag with a Guernsey cow on it, a puffin, and a Guernsey coaster.

I noticed as I looked at my phone missed calls from Elliott and Hayley. I don't know what had happened to my phone but I'd never heard it and it had been in my hand taking photos!

It had given them a bit of a scare though because they couldn't get me.

"I was getting close to the time I nearly bashed your door down when your phone had been off!" Elliott told me when I got back and went to them at the pool.

"I can't think why it never rang," I said, "unless I was ringing the taxi."

"Have you had a nice time?"

"I have thank you, lovely. A lovely trip down memory lane and a sit on the seafront, and a few treats from Guernsey Gifts."

"That's good then. Hayley has booked a table at The Deerhound for tea later. We'll go in two runs and come back for you so you don't have to have taxis."

"OK then that's good. I'll go and have a rest now."

We had a lovely carvery at The Deerhound and Hayley did the driving. I was well and truly whacked but it had been the most perfect day.

Plus I thought I'd got pictures of the seafront and Havelet Bay that I could use for my book covers. They would be lovely for the memories both old and new.

Day 5
Monday 11th August
Cobo Bay

To steal the words of Her Majesty Queen Elizabeth II in her 1992 annus horribilis speech, our beach day at Cobo is not one I shall remember with undiluted pleasure!

It all started off well enough. We set off, me in the taxi, Elliott, Hayley and children behind, well I thought they were. With hindsight I should have asked the taxi driver to wait and let them follow him so that they could see where he dropped me off, but hindsight is a wonderful thing. They must have been a way behind because they were nowhere to be seen when we got there.

I paid the driver and asked where to book to be picked up from later.

"Just ask for Mim's kiosk," he told me, "they'll know where you mean."

"OK thanks."

I got out and looked for Elliott but couldn't see them so I had a look around and took a few photos of the rugged coastline, spectacular rocks between sea and sand. Lots of young people wearing wet suits were preparing for their water sports. I had no idea what they were; it all looked far too energetic for me and all their young bodies looking fit and healthy performing in a way that mine had long forgotten how to.

I needed to sit down somewhere to wait for Elliott and family but so that they could see me, but where? All that there was were rocks at the back of the car park and would they notice me from the road? We'd passed a bigger car park which I'd thought we'd stop on but the taxi driver knew best or so I thought so I bowed to his greater knowledge and kept my mouth shut believing E&H were behind us. I ledged on the rocks and waited… and waited… I'm not good with no back support or even on upright chairs, M.E symptoms, muscles go weak so I hoped they wouldn't be long. I thought I saw them drive past but wasn't sure what the car was like other than it was black. If it had been them they'd come back surely? They did, and drove straight past.

Oh nooo! I could have wept. My back was now starting to become weak, not a good sign, and I still had to get to the beach even after they'd found me. I couldn't move because I'd no idea where they were, all I could do was wait and hope.

"We couldn't find you," a little voice said, coming over the hill beside me as Charlotte and Elliott at last did track me down from where they'd parked on the larger car park.

We all explained our predicament and went onto the beach to join Hayley and Harry. Charlotte bless her little heart carried my beach bag which was nearly as big as her as I could barely put one foot in front of the other.

It was a lovely beach, a wide expanse of golden sand but I felt too ill to appreciate its beauty. The shimmering sea sparkled in the sunlight and I had so looked forward to dipping my toes in the shallow waves, I'd never thought I'd ever see the sea again and never in Guernsey but I couldn't manage the walk to it even though it wasn't that far out; everything had now gone weak and all I wanted was to lie down.

They have a little beach tent for if it's too hot but that wasn't the case that day, it was fairly cloudy but not cold and at least as I was sitting/lying beside it, it enabled them all to go down to the sea for a paddle, which Harry loved! He wasn't too keen on the pool at the apartments, perhaps too cold or deep but the gentle waves lapping round his toes was quite warm Elliott said and it was just right for him.

I scooped a handful of sand to take back with me and put it into an empty sandwich bag along with a few shells Charlotte had found for me; a little memento, Guernsey sand and shells.

As well as watching my family enjoying the sea I watched the antics of a few seagulls strutting around looking for scraps. Two of them had a bit of a scuffle and I took a few pictures to send to a friend who had befriended one at her local Costa. It also reminded me of a reel on Facebook from Guernsey that someone had put together of a seagull following her around town on her lunchbreaks to the tune of Rockwell, 'Somebody's Watching Me,' very clever.

It was pleasant eating our picnic but then I thought I'd better ring for a taxi back because I needed a rest.

The next problem, my phone said no network connection! Good job it hadn't said that in St Peter Port the day before!

"Don't panic, we'll ring from mine," Elliott said.

Ten minutes the lady said so I made my way back to the rocks by Mim's kiosk. I noticed some beautiful delicate pink and white flowers growing in the grass, like tiny surfinias, but I hadn't got the energy to get my phone out to take a picture – now I wish I had – and I didn't want to miss the taxi, I needed to get back and soon. Once again I waited… and waited… Elliott had come with me thank goodness because my weak back was getting weaker with every minute that passed and I was trying to keep the lid on the anxiety. If that got out and ran amok I was doomed for sure.

People with no understanding of M.E weakness would have no clue at the all consuming fatigue that is experienced. It's not normal fatigue and tiredness, it's like every drop of energy has been sucked from every cell and mine were almost empty by that point.

"Can you ring again to see where it is?" I asked Elliott after twenty minutes had passed and still no sign of a taxi.

He did and was told another ten minutes! I was nearly dead!

At last it arrived and I fell into it. I didn't know whether I wanted to cry or die.

We followed a bus that stopped at every stop and I wilted further and further into the back seat like one of those tiny flowers would have done had I picked it.

"Oh I'll just turn round here and go back up the road," the driver told me as he'd made a wrong turn.

"OK," I answered, "I haven't a clue where we are."

At last we got back to the apartments, I paid him, got to my door and let myself in. I just wanted to collapse on the bed and die. I had to grab some sort of drink and snack first though for energy.

After resting a while I checked my phone for emails and was delighted to find one from Sam at the travel agents with my boarding pass for Wednesday; I just wanted to go home.

A couple of hours later as I felt a little better I did think that at least I had managed a beach day if not the paddle in the sea.

Before the holiday a Facebook meme had said words to the effect of 'Don't wait until you're better to live your life, you could be waiting forever. Do it anxious, Do it sad, Sometimes it's the experience that heals.'

I also found out what to do about the phone saying no network connection, by googling it. Turn flight mode on and off so it searches for a signal. Bingo!

Day 6
Tuesday 12th August
Rest Day

A more positive day today. I was glad of the rest. Showered and hair washed and I packed as I went along.

Elliott, Hayley and the children were going to Saumarez Park which I'd seen online but there was no way I could manage and it would be nice for them to go as a family; I was just looking forward to a quiet day.

They called in to me for a coffee, tea for me, before they went. Charlotte had a look into the bag of chocolates I'd bought from Rebecca's Chocolates that were on the coffee table, as she had every time they'd called in.

"I do like these chocolates," she repeated. "Are they all for your friends?"

We adults grinned to each other over her head.

"No," I answered, "they're for some people who have helped me with this holiday."

"We've helped you."

"I know. You've helped me a lot haven't you."

"Yes. I really like them." She closed the bag and went after Harry with his dinosaurs.

Off they went and left me to my packing.

I got a text from Steve's Travel who took me to Manchester airport to say his brother Brian who'd taken me would be there to pick me up tomorrow and then Brian himself texted a few minutes later to say he'd be there. I'd be ready to kiss his feet after that forty minute wait yesterday!

10.22 a.m. 22! It haunts me. If I've seen one car number

plate with 22 or 222 while we've been here I must have seen twenty. For the last few years those numbers have followed me everywhere: times, car registrations, Facebook shares, minutes, you name it if 22 or 222 can get in anywhere it does. Angel numbers a friend said so I googled it. 'Your angels are supporting you, you're on the right path.' To where? I'm seventy for goodness sake. How much of a path have I got left? There was a meme on Facebook a few years ago that said start a whole new life at seventy and sometimes that sounds good but then sometimes I just feel as though I'm galloping towards death. What game are the angels playing with all these twos I'd like to know and why have they followed me to Guernsey? There were two on Waitrose car park the first day we got here! Oh well, *que sera sera.*

When Elliott, Hayley and the children got back later in the afternoon I went and sat by the pool for while with them while Elliott and Charlotte had their last swim of the holiday and the rest of us made the most of the sun. It was just pleasantly warm, 22-24 degrees, Emily had said it was hot at home, 30 degrees. It seemed unimaginable. My packing was all done, case locked, only the last minute items to go in the hand luggage in the morning now.

Day 7
Wednesday 13th August
Home

Thanks to a sleeping pill I'd had a decent sleep and woke early, dressed and ready. Debbie who had greeted us came and asked if I'd like her to take my luggage up to Tracey's office, which was lovely of her and saved a lot of energy for me. The taxi was on time and we arrived at the airport early. There was a bit of frisking but not as invasive as Manchester! This time it was a much kinder older lady who apologized, unlike the hatched faced young Gestapo woman at Manchester who seemed to be enjoying her job rather more than necessary with a liberal amount of sadism! Old women and children must be used as drug mules is all I can think!! Charlotte thought it was fun! We had a half hour delay which turned into about forty five minutes by the time we boarded and were informed it was because someone on the previous flight had broken a door on the overhead locker and it had had to be fixed but eventually we were ready. I had the correct seat this time behind Elliott and Charlotte and I videoed our take off.

'Á la perchoine' Guernsey – until next time, although I don't know if there'll be a next time as I'm seventy and old but then look at Karen's parents, ninety, so you can never say never. Who knows?

I loved the flight as I had on the one to Guernsey. It was a bit disappointing initially as we were in cloud and I did think how could the pilot see where he was going but I suppose they go by instrument panels. There was a bit of turbulence when we were told to put on our seat-belts and Hayley and Elliott exchanged worried glances but I just thought it was like being on a bumpy road; it didn't worry me too much. We were through it soon enough and above the clouds to beautiful blue skies with wonderful puffball formations below us that I just had to get a photo of. I'd liked to have watched as we crossed the channel but that was when we were in cloud, when it cleared we were over land and again I'd have liked to have known where we were. At one point I thought I could see water to the left and I wondered if it was the Bristol Channel but I had no idea really, I was only guessing. I loved every little thing about it, the tilt of the wings and I had to look through the window every time, even videoed them and the propellor; I'll be watching it for months!

Soon the pilot announced that we were approaching Manchester and starting our descent so I got my phone ready to video the landing. I'd loved seeing all the buildings looking like tiny toys below, their rooves sparkling in the bright sunshine, the roads looking like ribbons, this whole new fantastic experience for this old girl.

I didn't know it at that point but Brian my taxi driver had said he'd seen us come in as he was waiting to pick me up, such a comforting thought.

The landing was soft and gentle, barely a bump, what an expert pilot. It was wonderful to taxi past the larger planes and everyone has said, 'Oh you'll want to go on a big jet next,' but I don't, I love those little Aurigny planes and the only place I ever want to go is Guernsey.

When we got off the plane the heat hit us. 30 degrees

Emily had said it was and it was so hot! Guernsey had been a comfortable 22-24 and cloudy as we'd left, Manchester and Stoke-on-Trent were baking hot!

Once again the airport assistance was impeccable, everyone carried my bag, and a minibus was waiting just for me! I asked if my family could come too as opposed to going on the shuttle bus as we were on the tarmac and we were asked how many of us there were. Five. That was fine.

It seemed as the Channel Islands are British there was no passport control as Hayley was expecting and she said could take ages so we were through in no time. Elliott took me outside to where Brian was waiting and we said our goodbyes. It had all gone wonderfully well.

It's always lovely to get home isn't it and after a welcome cup of tea and a rest and still surprised how baking hot it was, but it was great to return from a holiday to lovely weather, I took the luggage upstairs and just opened the case and carry on, didn't do much else.

I thought of my lovely M.E friend in the Facebook group who would post me the washing pussycat gif for my task the next day, thank goodness the weather was good!

I had Dido's 'Sand in my Shoes,' running through my head, 'I'll leave it until tomorrow to unpack.' The song is about a holiday romance but none of that for me this time, too old for all of that stuff and I wouldn't have wanted to meet someone who I really liked only to lose them because we were from different worlds, done that once.

Funny though, it only takes one moment to meet someone special and you never know do you regardless of age but I've no desire to go down the marriage route again after the last fiasco.

As my divorced friend says, I live with the best company, my own. I said this to a clairvoyant some years ago and she replied, 'Yes but we all need a bit of company.' Maybe she was right but it would depend on whose company; they'd have to be pretty special.

So was I happy with my return to Guernsey? Yes and no. I hadn't expected to be able to do what I had as a teen due to age and a health condition so some of my expectations had been open ended. It had been lovely to remember old memories, retrace old steps, and make new memories with my family. They say you can never go back but my teenage memories were still intact, filed away in their rose coloured box to be dipped into in moments of nostalgia. My new memories of my grandchildren running up the garden to my door and my family coming in for morning tea and coffee equally precious. Watching them play 'What Time is it Mr Wolf,' with Elliott in the garden as I sat resting on my bed, priceless.

We'd all asked each other our favourite parts of the holiday and being with each other was a main, the pool every day for them, and I remembered Elliott's words to Hayley as he swam with Charlotte on the first day, 'Isn't this lovely,' my day in St Peter Port for me, and of course the flights, I absolutely LOVE LOVE LOVED them!

Ever since writing Over A Spitfire in 2016 I've wanted to fly so this holiday has been two ticks off my bucket list: returning to Guernsey and flying.

The downside was needing to use taxis and not being enough room in the car. That sapped my budgeted energy but I was glad I'd asked in the Facebook group about them earlier because at least I had some good contacts and IF – big if – I ever dare visit again on my own, I'll know what to do, where to go.

Guernsey people are the loveliest people, so friendly and helpful everywhere I went, whether in person on holiday or people I chat to online. In a weird way it was like coming home even after all those years. I read somewhere we all have a place we are drawn to and mine is definitely Guernsey even after that first visit.

All in all it's been a good holiday. Something I'm glad I've done that I never thought I would and it just goes to show you're never too old.

Life didn't begin at forty for me, it was halted by my illness. Perhaps it will have a kickstart at seventy.

Whether there will be a next time or not I don't know, but Guernsey… you are forever in my heart.

❖

Thank you for reading this book.

If you have enjoyed it you may like a look at my other titles listed at the beginning. They include novels, series, short story and poetry collections and memoirs. More details can be found of the memoirs on the following pages.

Further details of all my work including A Sherry with Sherrie videos, interviews, events, photo gallery, can be found on my website

www.sherrielowe.co.uk

All are available from Amazon in ebook format and www.feedaread.com for the paperback copies.

Please don't buy used paperback copies of Shadow Across the Sun from Amazon as not only are they sold at extortionate prices, it was revised in 2021 for privacy reasons.

Other Memoirs

Shadow Across the Sun

PLEASE DO NOT PURCHASE USED PAPERBACK COPIES OF THIS BOOK FROM AMAZON.

Not only are they sold at extortionate prices but it has been revised in 2021 for privacy reasons.

For paperback copies please go to:

https://www.feedaread.com/books/Shadow-Across-the-Sun-9781803021874.aspx

Thank you.

I had an idyllic childhood - the best, loving family, good friends, beautiful woodland to play in in a picturesque village with quaint cottage sweetshops in the Staffordshire Moorlands in the UK.

The only shadow over the scene was illness - always there, and Fate had a vicious blow to deal.

In 1967 when I was just twelve years old, my mum was diagnosed with breast cancer. Following a mastectomy she received treatment for the rest of that year and into the next. The outcome wasn't what we hoped for however and we lost her in February 1968.

Someone at school told me about ouija boards. Desperate for contact with my mum my sister and I tried it. We were successful and it gave me my belief in the afterlife, a theme that is present in some of the novels I've written since.

You may purchase the eBook here.

https://www.amazon.co.uk/Shadow-Across-Sun-Sherrie-Lowe-ebook/dp/B007V42ON4

Better or Dead

eBook - https://www.amazon.co.uk/Better-Dead-Sherrie-Lowe-ebook/dp/B00JNS6TRS

Paperback - https://www.feedaread.com/books/Better-or-Dead-9781784075842.aspx

Every life has shades of dark and light and sometimes we all need a little help from a higher power. As I approached my 40th birthday my life was in the light for the first time in many years of various hues, then as ill health had plagued my family in the past, it came for me.

Life begins at forty so they say. Mine didn't. It ended.

M.E. also known as chronic fatigue syndrome (C.F.S.) is a very controversial illness for which there is no diagnostic test – diagnosis at present is by a process of elimination – no treatment and no cure. It is shrouded with disbelief and prejudice.

At a time when I should have been enjoying my life I faced an uphill struggle with a fight on my hands to survive, when I was too ill to fight.

This is my story.

My Furry Loves

Our pets play a huge role in our lives, our fur babies and grandbabies. Anyone who has ever loved an animal will know how unique and special each one is.

This is a memoir of every animal who has ever been a part of my life. Most of them are featured in my two human memoirs Shadow Across the Sun and Better or Dead but I thought they deserved their own book with lots of photographs to preserve them in time. My fur grandsons aren't in the other two memoirs so this is their first outing and I've given them a few words of their own.

Here they are, my furry loves.

Both eBook and paperback are available from Amazon as they contain colour photographs.

You may purchase a copy here:

https://www.amazon.co.uk/My-Furry-Loves-animal-memoir-ebook/dp/B08T5XW9ZF

Sherrie Lowe is a divorced mum and nanna living in Staffordshire UK. She began writing seriously when she became ill with M.E in 1995, after having to resign from her job as learning support assistant in a mainstream high school because she was too ill to continue. M.E, also called chronic fatigue syndrome is a little understood, debilitating illness that destroys lives. Writing has kept her sane through the loneliness and isolation that are a part of this condition.

On the positive side she had time on her hands and developed an interest in writing. When she was well enough she attended a creative writing class and learned to write fiction. To date she has published 22 books as memoirs, novels and short story collections.

Visit the author's website:
www.sherrielowe.co.uk

Follow Sherrie Lowe on X:
@SherrieLowe2

Printed in Dunstable, United Kingdom

71832834R00063